Series authors:
Malcolm Mann
Steve Taylore-Knowles

Laser B2

Workbook with key

MACMILLAN

Macmillan Education
4 Crinan Street
London N1 9XW
A division of Macmillan Publishers Limited
Companies and representatives throughout the world

ISBN 978-0-230-43385-4 (with Answer key)
978-0-230-43386-1 (without Answer key)

Series authors: Malcolm Mann & Steve Taylore-Knowles

This edition published 2013
Second edition published 2008
First edition published 2004

Original design by Peter Burgess
Page make-up by Red Giraffe
Illustrated by Oxford Designers & Illustrators
Cover design by Peter Burgess
Picture research by Alison Prior

The authors and publishers would like to thank the following for permission to reproduce their photographs:
Alamy/AceStock Ltd p113(t), Alamy/Jon Arnold Images p116(t), Alamy/Loetscher Chlaus p113(b), Alamy/Paul Doyle p31(l), Alamy/Editorial p63, Alamy/Eightfish p48,Alamy/Franky 242 p23, Andrew Fox p114(b), Alamy/INSADCO p31 (r), Alamy/B O'Kane p53(r), Alamy/Jonathan Larsen p61, Alamy/ONOKY-Photononstop p69, Alamy/David Pearson p114(t), Alamy/Phovoi p38(c), Alamy/Redsanpper p119(t), Alamy/Ian Shaw p119(b), Alamy/Martin Thomas Photography p116(b), Alamy/Wildlife GmbH p116(c), Alamy/Janine Wiedel Photography p100; **Corbis**/Martyn Goddard p77, Corbis/David P Hall p38(b), Corbis/Rob Lewine p38(t), Corbis/Gideon Mendel p14, Corbis/Ingo Wagner/dpa p92; **Eyewire** p53(l); **Getty Images** p31(c); **Image Source** pp7, 87.

Printed and bound in Thailand

2017 2016 2015 2014
10 9 8 7 6 5 4 3 2

Contents

1

Relationships

Reading 1: vocabulary

1 Match each word or phrase 1–8 with a meaning a–h.

1 approach ___	**a** experience
2 key ___	**b** usual, normal
3 criticism ___	**c** ask, require
4 face ___	**d** responsible
5 typical ___	**e** disapproval
6 to blame ___	**f** arise, appear
7 demand ___	**g** contact
8 come up ___	**h** important

2 Write a word or phrase from the box in each gap to complete the sentences.

perfectly balanced • anger • saying • rough patch • hurtful • annoy • in common • argument

1 His comments about my clothes were really ______________.
2 Don't expect everything to be ______________ even in a good relationship.
3 One ______________ worth remembering is: 'you can lead a horse to water, but you can't make it drink'.
4 We soon found out that we don't have a lot ______________.
5 They seem to be going through a ______________ at the moment.
6 They had a terrible ______________ and aren't speaking to each other.
7 He has some habits that really ______________ me!
8 He shouted at her in ______________ and later regretted it.

3 Choose the word or phrase (a, b or c) that is closest in meaning to the key phrase.

1 take it out on
a get angry with **b** have an argument **c** become jealous

2 take a deep breath
a be upset **b** pause **c** lose control

3 sort things out
a solve a problem **b** make arrangements **c** divide into groups

E Use of English: exam practice

Read the text below and think of the word which best fits each gap. Use only one word in each gap. Write your answers IN CAPITAL LETTERS.

Big Brothers and Big Sisters

Big Brothers and Big Sisters is an organisation (1) __________ supports children and teenagers aged from seven to seventeen. Children, and especially teenagers, need to have honest and caring relationships (2) __________ adults who can guide and help (3) __________ . Some children do not have strong role models in (4) __________ families, or for other reasons are not able to spend quality time with responsible adults. Because of this, social workers sometimes recommend children go (5) __________ *Big Brothers and Big Sisters*. (6) __________ child who comes to the organisation is matched (7) __________ a 'big brother' or 'big sister'. This person (8) __________ take an active interest in the child's life (9) __________ a long time. They spend time together, (10) __________ fun and sometimes doing exciting things. Most importantly, the big brother or big sister will listen (11) __________ the child or teenager and try to help him or her grow into a happy young adult. *Big Brothers and Big Sisters* (12) __________ established more than 100 years ago in New York and now has organisations throughout the world. It has made a big difference to a lot of young people!

E Reading: exam practice

You are going to read a magazine article about friendship. Seven sentences have been removed from the article. Choose from the sentences A–H the one which fits each gap (1–7). There is one extra sentence which you do not need to use.

A They spent all their weekends together, and several evenings a week too.

B There is much less time each day and each week to 'feed' the friendship, to prevent it from dying.

C For one production, she and another woman called Carol had to work very closely together on the script.

D It's actually very difficult to sustain this number of friends into adulthood.

E Because of this, I'm now much more careful about the friends I choose.

F They enjoy each other's company while they're working together, but they don't really socialise outside of the working environment.

G Real friends are actually incredibly hard to find.

H For this way of viewing friendship to be successful, it requires both people in the relationship to feel the same way about the other person.

A friend in need …

It's fairly easy to define what a relative is. It's a person you're biologically related to, or who has married someone you are biologically related to, or has been adopted, for example, by someone you're biologically related to. In short, it's someone in your family. It's not quite so easy to define what a friend is.

On an obvious level, our friends are people who are not family members whose company we enjoy. However, what about two people who work closely together in an office? [1] Are they friends, or just colleagues? And consider two people who were best friends at school, but haven't been in contact with each other for over 20 years. Are they still friends? Or should we say they used to be friends but aren't anymore?

'So what?', you might say. 'Perhaps friendship is tricky to define, but that doesn't matter. If you think you're friends with someone then you are, but if you don't then you're not.' In many cases, that might be a good general rule, but there are potential problems with it. [2] There are countless examples of relationships where that doesn't happen.

Take Jane, for example. She joined an amateur dramatics club, which puts on plays two or three times a year. [3] They met several times a week, and frequently called each other on the phone. As Jane says, 'I enjoyed working with Carol, and we got on well together. It was really difficult when we'd finished the play, though. Carol still wanted to meet up and chat regularly. I didn't, mainly because I just didn't have time. I've got a family and a busy social life, and I wasn't looking for any more close friends. How do you tell someone who thinks they're your close friend that really they're not?'

A further problem is the issue of 'fair-weather friends'. These are people who you consider to be your friends, but prove themselves not to be when things get tough. Jake, for example, thought that Dave was a really close friend. 4 ___ They both shared an interest in movies, and had the same sense of humour. 'Everything was great,' says Jake, 'until my mother became ill. It was a troubling time for me, and I got a bit depressed. I needed Dave to give me some support, but he wasn't interested. He just disappeared.' What Jake needed, and what Dave was not, was the kind of friend referred to in the saying 'a friend in need is a friend indeed'. The idea behind this is that if you are still the friend of someone when they are 'in need', when they need something such as help from you, then you are a real friend. You're not a 'fair-weather friend'. 5 ___ Most adults say that they only have two or three real friends – people they can totally rely on in difficult times. At school, children and teenagers often have one or two 'best friends', but they also have a wide circle of other friends – 20 or 30 is not uncommon. 6 ___ The main reasons for this are time and shared experience. Children see their friends every day (during term time) and have plenty of opportunity to 'feed' the friendship – in class, during the breaks, after school. Also, of course, all the members of the group live close together, and have a shared interest (the school and what happens there). With adults, this is rarely possible. 7 ___ And, of course, people move apart geographically when they grow up, and lose the sense of a shared interest when they start working in different fields, or spending their time in different ways. Very few of our friends from school remain real, close friends 20 years later.

V Vocabulary

1 Choose the correct word to complete the sentences.

1 This book is so **bored / boring** that every time I start reading it, I fall asleep!
2 My mum thinks classical music is very **relaxed / relaxing**, but I can't stand it!
3 Monica was very **frightened / frightening** by the horror movie she saw last night.
4 All my friends are **excited / exciting** about the party this weekend.
5 I find football **tired / tiring**. I prefer indoor sports like table tennis.
6 My little brother can be a bit **annoyed / annoying** sometimes – particularly when he won't be quiet!
7 I'm not very **interested / interesting** in science, but I love maths.

2 Use a form of the words in brackets in each gap to complete the sentences.

1 You shouldn't have spoken so ____________ (**rude**) to the shop assistant.
2 Many teenagers pay a lot of attention to their ____________ (**appear**).
3 The new boy in my class looks rather shy and speaks ____________ (**nervous**).
4 We've got some ____________ (**relate**) staying for the weekend.
5 Margo ____________ (**friend**) me on the first day I went to my new school.
6 Your ____________ (**jealous**) is making it hard for us to remain friends.

3 Match each word or phrase 1–7 with a phrasal verb a–g.

1 raise	___	**a**	let down
2 get older	___	**b**	split up
3 be like	___	**c**	grow up
4 take care of	___	**d**	take after
5 tolerate	___	**e**	bring up
6 end a relationship	___	**f**	put up with
7 disappoint	___	**g**	look after

4 Write a word from the box in each gap to complete the sentences.

selfish • nervous • honest • polite • alone • kind • funny • lonely

1 I was so ____________ the first time I went out with Kylie, my hands were shaking!
2 Sue thought the film was very ____________ and laughed out loud the whole time.
3 I rather like being ____________ ; I enjoy the peace and quiet.
4 Children tend to be ____________ . They don't really want to share their things.
5 It's not ____________ to interrupt when someone else is talking.
6 Since Pat moved away from her friends, she's been feeling rather ____________ .
7 John is a very ____________ person who always helps people in need.
8 Bob borrowed my favourite CD without asking me and then denied it. He's not very ____________ .

Reading 2: vocabulary

1 Match each word 1–6 with a meaning a–f.

1 childish	___	**a** very painful and upsetting	
2 miserable	___	**b** tolerable	
3 sympathetic	___	**c** immature	
4 traumatic	___	**d** without thinking first	
5 bearable	___	**e** unhappy	
6 impulsive	___	**f** understanding	

E Use of English: exam practice

Read the text below and decide which answer (A, B, C or D) best fits each gap.

Friendship

One thing adults, and especially parents, don't always understand is that friendships are a (1) ___________ part of teenagers' lives. As young people (2) ___________ and become more independent, the more they (3) ___________ to spend time out with friends. One (4) ___________ problem is when parents decide to move to a new area because of work. This can be a very upsetting (5) ___________ for teenagers. They are bound to feel (6) ___________ and this is likely to make them (7) ___________, too. It may take some time for them to develop new relationships, so parents should be patient. They should also try to be (8) ___________ about how much time teenagers spend with their friends. It's natural for teenagers to want to be out when they can. If they hear only (9) ___________ of their behaviour, it is likely to lead to a lot of (10) ___________. Encourage teenagers to develop friendships with people they have something in (11) ___________ with. And remember that (12) ___________ is the best policy when it comes to talking to teens on any subject at all, including their friendships.

	A	B	C	D
1	**A** key	**B** right	**C** rough	**D** sympathetic
2	**A** bring up	**B** take up	**C** grow up	**D** look up
3	**A** claim	**B** act	**C** demand	**D** order
4	**A** official	**B** kind	**C** honest	**D** typical
5	**A** experiment	**B** experience	**C** exercise	**D** encounter
6	**A** bearable	**B** hurtful	**C** tempted	**D** lonely
7	**A** incompatible	**B** miserable	**C** jealous	**D** embarrassed
8	**A** relaxed	**B** scared	**C** bored	**D** annoyed
9	**A** anger	**B** saying	**C** objection	**D** criticism
10	**A** actions	**B** arguments	**C** approaches	**D** effects
11	**A** common	**B** face	**C** balance	**D** match
12	**A** honesty	**B** attraction	**C** jealousy	**D** obedience

G Grammar 2

1 Choose the correct word or phrase to complete the sentences.

1 I **have / had** been to Spain several times, so I know a few words of Spanish.
2 As soon as she **has / had** got her results, Gwen phoned her mother.
3 We **have / had** already finished doing the preparations when Dan arrived, late as usual.
4 Nick **has / had** only just left home when we got to the train station.
5 Andrea still **hasn't / hadn't** written me a letter and it's been six months!
6 Kristina and John **have / had** never travelled abroad before last summer.
7 You **have / had** been a great help to me lately. Thanks!
8 Once **I've / I'd** finished my homework, I'll help you with yours.

2 Use a form of the words in brackets in each gap to complete the sentences.

1 Gary's one of the best players this year. He ____________ (**be**) on the football team since he was very young.
2 I ____________ (**just / move**) here when I met Susie.
3 ____________ (**you / ever / have**) an argument that ended a friendship?
4 I ____________ (**have**) an argument with my best friend Mary when you saw me crying this morning.
5 Marcos and I ________________________! (**just / break up**)
6 Luke ____________ (**only / play**) in a couple of games before he was made team captain.

E Use of English: exam practice

1 Read the text below. Use the word given in capitals at the end of some of the lines to form a word that fits in the gap in the same line. Write your answers IN CAPITAL LETTERS.

Teenage Actors

Many young people are tempted by the idea of a career in (1) ____________.	**ACT**
It certainly looks like very (2) ____________ work, but it's not for everyone. The	**EXCITE**
rewards can be huge, but it can also be difficult to make a living. In order to be	
successful as an actor, you must be (3) ____________ and willing to learn new	**TALENT**
skills. It helps to be (4) ____________, but there's no need to be a super model!	**ATTRACT**
Many people who are not traditionally attractive have had success. An	
(5) ____________ face is what people want to see. Sometimes it also helps to look	**INTEREST**
a little (6) ____________ from the rest. It means that people who see you perform	**DIFFER**
will remember who you are. A (7) ____________ from a well-known acting	**QUALIFY**
school can be useful, but not all (8) ____________ is learned at school. Experience	**KNOW**
really counts! Taking part in performances is often more important than exam	
results. Beyond that, you have to be able to put up with (9) ____________ hours of	**TIRE**
rehearsals and some (10) ____________ along the way. If you can do all that, you	**DISAPPOINT**
just might become a star!	

2 Complete the second sentence so that it has a similar meaning to the first sentence, using the word given. Do not change the word given. You must use between two and five words, including the word given. Write the missing words IN CAPITAL LETTERS.

1 Getting over a break-up can take some time.
recover
It can take some time ______ a break-up.

2 Ed and Stacey got married in September.
been
Ed and Stacey ______ September.

3 Marie started acting six years ago.
for
Marie ______ six years.

4 James Dean grew up in Indiana with his aunt and uncle.
raised
James Dean ______ his aunt and uncle in Indiana.

5 I have tolerated your behaviour for too long!
put
I ______ your behaviour for too long!

6 I solved the problem quickly with Jack's help.
out
Jack helped ______ the problem quickly.

7 I tried talking to her a few days ago.
already
I ______ talking to her.

8 I saw Steve right after he took his exams.
just
Steve ______ his exams when I saw him.

E Listening: exam practice

CD Track 1 You will hear people talking in five different situations. For questions 1–5, choose the best answer (A, B or C).

1 You hear this man talking about his friend. What did they argue about?
A money
B a secret
C another friend

2 You hear this woman talking on the radio. What does she say about having a twin sister?
A It has never been a problem.
B It has advantages.
C It can sometimes be embarrassing.

3 You hear this man talking on the phone. Who is he talking to?
A his brother
B his boss at work
C his mother

4 You hear this woman talking about her son. How has their relationship changed recently?
A They are closer now.
B They argue more now.
C They communicate less now.

5 You hear these two people talking. What is their relationship?
A relatives
B colleagues
C acquaintances

2

Travelling

Reading 1: vocabulary

1 Use a word from the box in each gap to complete the sentences.

freedom • crackling • swears • checked • secluded

1 She warmed her hands by the __________ fire.
2 The farmhouse is very __________ and you won't be disturbed.
3 Being out in the countryside on horseback gave me a real sense of __________.
4 A red and white __________ cloth covered the kitchen table.
5 The woman __________ she had nothing to do with the robbery.

2 Use a word or phrase from the boxes in each gap to complete the sentences.

get bored • excitement • ultimate

1 If you are looking for a holiday with a bit more __________ than usual, then call us at Zenith Travel and we will make sure you find the __________ holiday experience where you won't __________ for a second.

adventure • saddle • streams • itching to • trails • tracked

2 I was __________ go on some kind of __________, so I got in the __________ and went on a riding trip down one of the Wild West __________ – we also __________ deer in the woods and went fly fishing in the __________.

valley • porch • cabin

3 We stayed in a lovely log __________ with a small front __________ where we'd sit to admire the view of the __________ below.

sheer • keep you busy • enjoy yourself

4 You'll really __________ on the farm and you'll be impressed by the __________ beauty of the scenery; but they will __________, so you'll be tired at the end of each day.

G Grammar 1

1 Choose the correct word or phrase to complete the sentences.

1 Please will you turn the music down while I **drive / am driving**?
2 I **was packing / packed** my suitcases when I suddenly remembered I had left my passport in my friend's room.
3 I am hot because I **sat / have been sitting** on a crowded bus for the last two hours.
4 Sarah only came back from Germany last week and she **already plans / is already planning** her next trip.
5 When I met Alex, I **was staying / have been staying** on a campsite for a few days.
6 When the bus arrived, I realised that the taxi driver **has been lying / had been lying** to us.

2 Use a verb from the box in the correct form in each gap to complete the sentences.

go • drive • travel • do • look • stay

1 What worried me most was the fact that we __________ a car which was not suitable for those roads.
2 We __________ in the Carlton Hotel – come and see us if you get the chance.
3 We __________ for four days when Paul fell ill.
4 Martin and I __________ at brochures and we think we've decided where we want to go this year.
5 What __________ yesterday evening at around 8 o'clock? I phoned to talk about the school trip but there was no answer.
6 The bus was going through a tunnel when suddenly the lights __________ out.

3 Use the verbs given to complete the dialogue. Use present (simple or continuous), present perfect (simple or continuous) and past (simple or continuous) tenses.

Interviewer: I have with me in the studio Laura Macdonald. Laura, you (1) __________ (**travel**) around the world in rather an unusual way for the last six months, haven't you?

Laura: That's right. I (2) __________ (**try**) to get around the world for free for the last six months, and I'm about halfway there. I (3) __________ (**rest**) for the last few days, but I (4) __________ (**leave**) again tomorrow.

Interviewer: So you (5) __________ (**do**) it for free. How does that work?

Laura: Well, about a year ago I (6) __________ (**sit**) at home and my husband and I (7) __________ (**watch**) a documentary about going round the world. I (8) __________ (**want**) to do that, but I couldn't afford it. Then I (9) __________ (**have**) the idea that you could do it for free, and that's what I (10) __________ (**do**) now.

Interviewer: What inspired you to try such a thing?

Laura: It's only the actual travel that I (11) __________ (**try**) to get for free. I have some money to pay for food and accommodation, but I (12) __________ (**pay**) for a single ticket so far. I (13) __________ (**rely**) on people's generosity and you'd be surprised to learn how much people help. I've had lifts in cars, on bicycles, and even in a private plane!

Interviewer: That's amazing. Now, tell us about the time you (14) __________ (**travel**) through China and you had an accident.

Laura: Well, it's a long story. First of all, …

4 There are six mistakes with tenses in the following text. Find the mistakes and rewrite them correctly.

went

At my last school, we ~~were going~~ on a summer trip to a campsite by the sea every year. One year, however, I remember being more excited than usual. I think it was because my best friends, Joanne and Michelle, were promising that they would meet me there. On the morning of the day we had been leaving, I looked forward to the trip – and seeing my friends of course – when Joanne came round and told me that there had been a change of plan and they couldn't come. She is calling my mobile for days, but I had changed my phone and I had forgotten to tell her the new number. I was miserable for the whole week – and all because I was making a stupid mistake.

E Reading: exam practice

You are going to read an article from the travel section of a newspaper. For questions 1–8, choose the answer (A, B, C or D) which you think fits best according to the text.

1 When the writer advises people not to go on holiday, she
A is being dishonest.
B is just joking.
C really means it.
D is being unkind.

2 According to the writer, airports are
A expensive.
B difficult to get to.
C badly organised.
D difficult to find.

3 The writer uses the phrase 'a short hop' (line 23) to describe
A a journey that isn't very long.
B tropical tourist resorts.
C how many hours a journey takes.
D the possibility of airport delays.

4 The writer thinks that a two-week holiday
A is a good opportunity to go to museums.
B can help you learn a new language.
C isn't long enough to learn about a country.
D gives people a chance to meet other tourists.

5 The word 'they' (line 51) refers to
A package holidays.
B tourists.
C local communities.
D holiday companies.

6 The writer says that mass tourism
A benefits local people.
B is a good way to travel cheaply.
C has few benefits.
D is a way of stealing tourists' money.

7 The writer says that most people
A would prefer longer holidays.
B are unable to go on long holidays.
C spend months in another country.
D learn about a country before visiting it.

8 On the whole, the writer believes that people should
A never travel abroad.
B only travel if they have to.
C take holidays in their own country.
D avoid mass tourism.

Don’t go on Holiday!

Dawn Lanare takes a good look at some of the reasons not to travel this summer.

Yes, I’m being completely serious. Travel can broaden the mind but that’s not likely on a two-week holiday. Let me tell you why.

It’s summertime again and you’re planning to pack your bags and take off for a package holiday for two weeks in the sun. It’s a chance to relax, recharge your batteries and enjoy yourself. But if you’re honest with yourself, is it really such a good idea? Think about all the holidays you’ve had in the past few years. What were they really like?

For a start, there is the stress of travelling. The actual getting to and returning from our chosen destination is usually stressful and tiring. Airports are always in the middle of nowhere and take hours to get to. It’s also expensive to get to them, too. Then there’s the fact that you have to be at the airport at least an hour before your departure, which adds more hours to all the travel. Let’s not forget, either, that
23 even **a short hop** to the nearest sunny resort is going to take at least a couple of hours and, during the main holiday season, delays and strikes can mean getting stuck at the airport. All too often, by the time you get to your holiday destination, you’ll be too tired and miserable to enjoy your first day there.

One of the reasons we convince ourselves that going abroad is a good idea is because we want to learn something about the place we’re going to visit. We might go sightseeing around museums and archaeological sites and we hope we will absorb some of the culture of the place while we’re there. But we’re just fooling ourselves. It simply isn’t possible to learn anything meaningful about a culture in just two weeks. We might learn a few words of the language and try some new food but we’re not even so much as scratching the surface of a country’s culture when we spend most of our time in a resort, sitting on a beach with hundreds of other tourists.

Another white lie we tell ourselves is that at least we’re helping the local economy by going on holiday. The bitter truth is that you probably aren’t. If you’re on a package holiday, then very little of your money goes to local people. Most of the profits will go to the companies that run
the resorts and **they** are, as you’ve probably 51
guessed, usually foreign-owned companies. Most tourists will spend very little money in the local community as their package holiday covers all their meals. So the only money that goes straight into the local economy is what you spend buying souvenirs or traditional craftworks from local people.

Now I don’t want to make you all feel too downhearted but there’s no getting away from facts. In short, mass tourism is of very little value to local communities and their environments. Package holidays are sold to us as a wonderful opportunity to see the world cheaply, but we are being cheated. We spend two weeks away from home in a resort where we will hardly get a chance to see what life in the country we are visiting is like and where our presence is more likely to do harm than good.

It’s not that I’m completely against all travel, not at all. What I’m against is the form of mass tourism that has developed in the 21st century. I think we should go back to the days when travel was a leisurely pursuit, when people would spend months getting to know a place, learning the language and soaking up the culture. Unfortunately, this form of travel isn’t possible for most of us as we only get a couple of weeks off in the summer. But if you ever do get the chance to really spend time in another country, then you should jump at it.

V Vocabulary

1 Choose the correct word or phrase.

1 Which of these is *not* related to trains?
a platform **b** ticket inspector **c** runway **d** carriage

2 Which of these is *not* related to boats?
a sail **b** rails **c** voyage **d** cabin

3 Which of these is *not* related to air travel?
a land **b** departure lounge **c** flight **d** ferry

2 Write one word in each gap to complete the sentences.

1 I'll call you when I get ________ from my holiday.
2 The one thing I hate about flying is the moment when the plane takes ________ .
3 You'll need to speed ________ if you want to get to London before dark.
4 Of course, we all wanted to go to the station to see my brother ________ .
5 Our flight was at seven o'clock but we had to check ________ at five.
6 Slow ________ – you're going much too fast!

3 Use a word from the box in each gap to complete the phrases.

trip • inhabitants • hotel • time • broaden • business

1 to go on a(n) ________ trip
2 the ________ of a place
3 to ________ the mind
4 to go on a school ________
5 a five-star ________
6 to take ________ off work

E Use of English: exam practice

Read the text below and decide which answer (A, B, C or D) best fits each gap.

British Holidaymakers

The traditional British holiday at home is not dead. In fact, it could be making a comeback. Because of worries about travelling abroad, many British people have decided to investigate (1) ___ a lot closer to home. Popular (2) ___ such as Brighton in the south and Scarborough or Blackpool in the north have never really lost their (3) ___ . However, some seaside towns, which until recently have struggled, are attracting more holidaymakers.

Once they get there, holidaymakers need to be able to get around. While the car is still preferred, the majority of tourists will try at least one other (4) ___ of transport during their holiday. Trains, for instance. Although few people would choose to start their two-week break by taking the (5) ___ train, a large number of them will enjoy the luxury of a restored wooden carriage on one of the many historical (6) ___ in operation around the country. And for those who do make it to the sea, many are tempted by a (7) ___ ride to nearby islands or a short (8) ___ on a pleasure boat. We may not be tempted by the prospect of a three-week (9) ___ to exotic and (10) ___ countries, but our love of the sea is clearly not lost.

However, a quick look inside the (11) ___ lounges of our major airports will confirm that we are still queuing up in our thousands to (12) ___ in for a flight in search of the one thing the British Isles cannot guarantee – sunshine.

	A	B	C	D
1	**A** reports	**B** arrivals	**C** cultures	**D** resorts
2	**A** destinations	**B** directions	**C** venues	**D** excursions
3	**A** popularity	**B** fame	**C** growth	**D** inhabitants
4	**A** way	**B** method	**C** means	**D** sort
5	**A** direct	**B** express	**C** rapid	**D** delayed
6	**A** platforms	**B** runways	**C** rails	**D** railways
7	**A** transport	**B** ferry	**C** sail	**D** ship
8	**A** run	**B** package	**C** cruise	**D** ticket
9	**A** voyage	**B** sail	**C** flight	**D** travel
10	**A** distant	**B** away	**C** further	**D** long
11	**A** departure	**B** going	**C** exit	**D** holiday
12	**A** book	**B** register	**C** check	**D** go

Reading 2: vocabulary

1 Choose the correct word or phrase to complete the sentences.

1 Every year, thousands of tourists __________ to the Mediterranean in search of sandy beaches.
a flock **b** vow **c** appeal

2 There is nothing like the feeling of skiing down the __________ of a mountain.
a glaciers **b** cable cars **c** slopes

3 You can find out about all sorts of holidays if you visit your __________ agent.
a secret **b** journey **c** travel

4 After the exams, why not __________ yourself to a weekend break?
a spend **b** treat **c** handle

5 We drove through some __________ scenery on the way to Vienna.
a spectacular **b** luxurious **c** comfortable

6 On some holidays, there's so much to see that you really need to have a(n) __________ guide to show you around.
a relaxed **b** experienced **c** wandering

2 Choose the correct word to complete the sentences.

1 This **region / neighbourhood** is world-famous for its glaciers.

2 You are **possible / bound** to meet some interesting people on your travels.

3 Many of the souvenirs that tourists bring home from here are small animals **carved / constructed** out of wood.

4 **Going / Getting** away from it all has never been easier with our new range of package holidays to suit every budget!

5 Being pulled across the ice on a dog **rink / sled** is a very unusual experience.

6 This **festival / culture** is held every year in June.

G Grammar 2

1 Use a word from the box in each gap to complete the sentences.

so • such • too • enough • used • would

1 When I was younger, my parents ____________ often take me away with them when they were travelling on business.
2 Some people find that it's just ____________ hot to do anything in the middle of the day.
3 This tour of Africa is ____________ expensive that only very rich people can afford to go on it.
4 It was ____________ a frightening experience that I vowed I would never do it again.
5 My parents had told me that they didn't have ____________ money for a summer holiday that year.
6 I ____________ to go to sleep imagining what it would be like to live in the exotic places I read about.

2 If a sentence is correct, put a tick (✔). If it is incorrect, rewrite it correctly.

1 I love being on holiday but I am not used to have so much free time.
2 The tickets were expensive enough so I couldn't go.
3 It was so a long and tiring journey that I was asleep when we arrived.
4 When we were there on holiday, I thought New Zealand was too interesting.
5 I will never get used to flying, however many times I do it.
6 When I was very young, we would live in Portugal.
7 It used to be much harder for people to have foreign holidays.
8 My sister is not enough old, so she'll have to wait until next year.

E Use of English: exam practice

1 Read the text below. Use the word given in capitals at the end of some of the lines to form a word that fits in the gap in the same line. Write your answers IN CAPITAL LETTERS.

SCHOOL HOLIDAYS

While this year's school holidays are still quite fresh in the memory, it is perhaps the best time to
begin making (1) ____________ for next year. Ask yourself how it went this year. Perhaps you only **PREPARE**
went as far as the (2) ____________ video shop to rent a film. If this sounds like you, now is the **NEAR**
time to consider your (3) ____________ for next year and there is a huge choice of organisations **OPT**
(4) ____________ for teenagers' tastes. Firstly, think about where you want to go. The first step in **CATER**
any holiday is deciding on a (5) ____________. Do you want to travel abroad? **LOCATE**
If so, it is usually cheaper to go on a (6) ____________ holiday. Then again, perhaps you are the **PACK**
kind of person who needs to be active on holiday. If you're the (7) ____________ type who likes **DOOR**
nothing more than a wide range of new and exciting (8) ____________ to try out, an adventure **ACTIVE**
holiday could be just the challenge you need. Above all, make sure you don't turn next year's
holiday into a struggle for (9) ____________. Having a good time can sometimes be an **SURVIVE**
(10) ____________ in itself. **ACHIEVE**

2 Complete the second sentence so that it has a similar meaning to the first sentence, using the word given. Do not change the word given. You must use between two and five words, including the word given. Write the missing words IN CAPITAL LETTERS.

1 I started going abroad when I was ten.
have
I ______________________ I was ten.

2 The holiday was so expensive that we could only afford one week.
an
It was ______________________ that we could only afford one week.

3 After Peter's visits, we would all say goodbye to him at the station.
see
After Peter's visits, we would all ______________________ at the station.

4 Hilda was too young to travel on her own.
enough
Hilda was ______________________ to travel on her own.

5 Years ago, a lot of people spent their holidays with relatives.
used
Years ago, a lot of people ______________________ their holidays with relatives.

6 I was promised the best holiday I had ever had but it turned out to be a disaster.
lifetime
I was promised ______________________ but it turned out to be a disaster.

7 One place that is becoming increasingly popular with teenagers is Canada.
destination
Canada is an ______________________ among teenagers.

8 Because we were so compatible, the trip was a great success.
got
Because we ______________________ well, the trip was a great success.

E Listening: exam practice

CD Track 2 You will hear an interview with a tour guide. For questions 1–5, complete the sentences.

The city of Perth was founded in (1) __________ .

Unlike Sydney, the first people to live in Perth weren't (2) __________ .

Many people (3) __________ in the coastal areas near the city.

The West Australian Art Gallery is a good place for exhibitions of (4) __________ .

The local cricket team, Australian rules football and (5) __________ teams are all popular.

3

Technology

Reading 1: vocabulary

1 Use a word or phrase from the box in each gap to complete the text.

apps • download • gadgets • mobile device • handy • notify

A smartphone is a (1) ______________ that is much more than just a phone. It has a whole variety of functions, depending on what kind of (2) ______________ you want to (3) ______________ on to it. For instance, my smartphone is very (4) ______________ when I want to find a location I'm looking for. I just use the GPS. Another thing it can do is (5) ______________ me when I have a meeting or appointment coming up. It's definitely the most useful of all the (6) ______________ I have.

2 For each word or phrase, write a word or phrase with a similar meaning. Some letters have been given to help you.

1 a program that allows you to speak to it v__________ r__________ t__________
2 watch, check mon__________
3 a program that helps you find pages on the internet s__________ e__________
4 feel proud of t__________ p__________ i__________
5 software that guesses the words you write p__________ t__________
6 developing, happening now unf__________

Grammar 1

1 If a sentence refers to the future, put a tick (✔).

1 My computer science class is in an hour. ____
2 Industrial technology is really very exciting! ____
3 Scientists are developing new technologies every day. ____
4 Our school is hosting a technology fair next month. ____
5 Do you think you might get an implant one day? ____
6 That might be your mobile phone over there. ____
7 Many machines will use sensors to recognise people. ____
8 The cash is going to be transferred automatically from your bank account. ____

2 Choose the correct phrase to complete the sentences.

1 In the year 2010, ________________ automatic payment systems instead of cash.
- **a** we'll be using
- **b** we're using
- **c** we use

2 By this time next year, our school ________ ________ iris sensors in the library!
- **a** will have installed
- **b** will have been installing
- **c** will install

3 In fifty years' time, ________________ with robots.
- **a** we are all living
- **b** we'll all have been living
- **c** we're all going to be living

4 By the end of today, scientists ________ ________ even more advances in technology.
- **a** will have been making
- **b** will have made
- **c** will make

3 Complete the sentences using *will*, *shall*, *be going to*, present continuous or present simple. If more than one choice is correct, write all choices.

1 Pretty soon ________ (**all computers / be**) wireless.

2 When I go to university, ________ (**I / study**) computer technology.

3 ________ (**I / help**) you choose a new laptop? I know all about them.

4 ________ (**Chris / really / go**) to the technology fair again this year?

5 Why ________ (**you / talk**) to your science teacher tomorrow about your idea?

6 One day, ________ (**people / communicate**) without using mobile phones.

4 Imagine it is Sunday evening. Read these pages from Francesca's diary.

Write five sentences about things Francesca *is doing* this week.

1 ________________

2 ________________

3 ________________

4 ________________

5 ________________

Write five sentences about things Francesca *will be doing* at particular times this week.

6 ________________

7 ________________

8 ________________

9 ________________

10 ________________

Write five sentences about things Francesca *will have done* by the end of this week.

11 ________________

12 ________________

13 ________________

14 ________________

15 ________________

November

Monday 12
call computer shop
go to gym
8pm dinner with Adrian

Tuesday 13
11am meeting with Tim about the office computers
shopping with Julie

Wednesday 14
9am work on website
12pm lunch with Adrian
go to gym

Thursday 15
2pm flight to Paris (Hotel Splendide)
6pm meeting at FranceTech

Friday 16
11am flight back to London

Saturday 17
go to gym
dinner with Adrian (book at Charlie's)

Sunday 18

E Reading: exam practice

You are going to read an article about social networking. Seven sentences have been removed from the article. Choose from the sentences A–H the one which fits each gap (1–7). There is one extra sentence which you do not need to use.

A We can now be online anytime and anywhere and it seems that's what many people want.

B It's likely that social networking will grow in other areas of our lives too.

C But this won't stop people from using the sites.

D Not many sensible people use them.

E It seems safe to say that they will continue to grow.

F They started out being mainly a way for people to keep in touch with friends and socialise while sitting at their computers.

G And they do have massive numbers of followers who hang onto their every word.

H One intriguing trend is that people are instantly blogging about important events in the world.

A New Trend Unfolds

Social networking and microblogging sites such as Facebook and Twitter might not have been around for very long but they've managed to have a huge impact on how we lead our lives. They've also become a major influence on the world of business, politics and journalism, too.

Why have these sites had such an impact? [1] But in recent years they have taken on a life of their own and it's now quite rare to find anyone who isn't involved in a networking site of some kind. The other strange thing is that people may have many thousands more friends and contacts in the virtual world than they do IRL (in real life).

Those who are critical of social networking say that people are becoming too involved in the internet. Some bosses have banned the sites on workplace computers because workers are spending too much time chatting or tweeting online. [2] That's because most will just carry on on their own personal smartphones or tablet pcs instead. There's not a lot employers can do about that. In fact, it's the rise in the use of portable smartphones and tablets that is one of the driving forces behind the demand for social networking. [3]

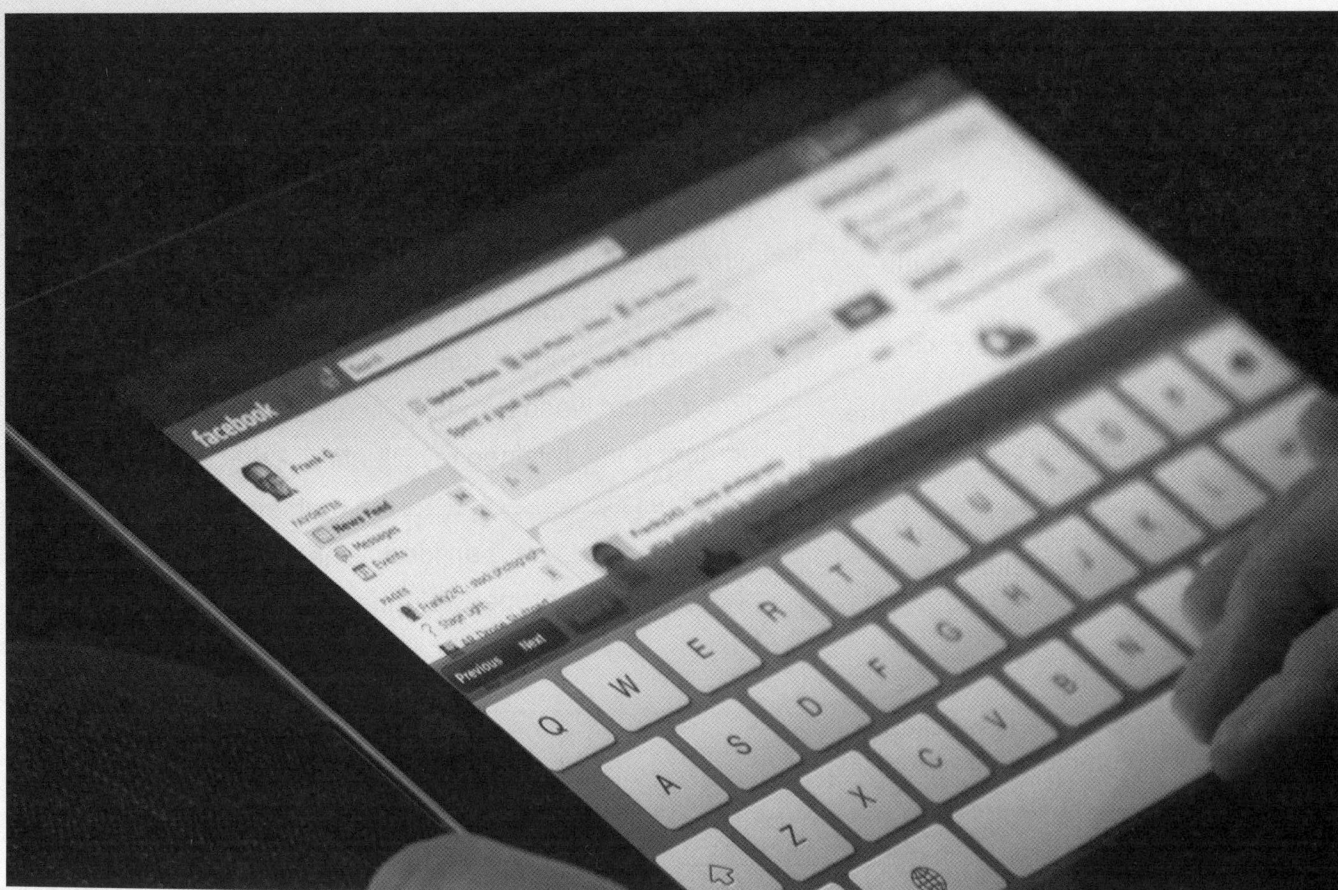

Another criticism is that social networking is affecting our culture, making us more obsessed with celebrities and destroying any form of private life we once had. It's certainly true that a lot of celebrities use Twitter as a form of publicity and to keep up their public profile. [4] There's also no doubt that some people using sites like Twitter give out too much information about their daily lives. Especially annoying are those people who can't seem to help tweeting every boring detail of everything they do.

But social networking sites are simply a tool and it's up to users to shape the way they are used. And quite a lot of what is happening on social networking and microblogging sites is both interesting and exciting. [5] From pictures from war zones to posting election results, microbloggers often get there much faster than professional journalists. This is why many media and news sites now use a lot of content from so-called 'citizen journalists'.

So what does the future hold for networking and microblogging sites? [6] But considering how much they have developed in such a short space of time, it isn't easy to predict exactly how they will develop in the future. One thing that seems sure is that they will spread even deeper into our culture. More and more businesses are using them to help promote their products and politicians to keep their face and ideas in voters' minds. [7] Whether this will be a good or bad thing depends on how we use it.

V Vocabulary

1 Match to make phrases.

1 light ____ a oven
2 alarm ____ b cooker
3 electric ____ c bulb
4 microwave ____ d cleaner
5 vacuum ____ e clock

2 Use a phrasal verb from the box in the correct form in each gap to complete the text.

break down • come up with • cut off get through • look into • put in

THE TROUBLE WITH COMPUTERS

I didn't think my brand new laptop could (1) ____________ already, but it seemed like it had. The first time I tried to connect to the internet I got (2) ____________ . The second time I tried, I couldn't (3) ____________ at all. The modem wasn't working. I called the technical support number and explained my situation. They told me they would (4) ____________ the problem. Then I (5) ____________ an idea. I checked to see if the phone line was properly plugged into the laptop, and once I (6) ____________ the line, I had no problem at all.

3 Use a form of the words in brackets in each gap to complete the sentences.

1 What was Alfred Nobel's greatest ____________ (**achieve**)?
2 I'd like to invent something that is ____________ (**benefit**) to people in developing countries, like a water purification system perhaps.
3 You're very ____________ (**create**). You should be an artist!
4 Recent ____________ (**develop**) in medicine are helping people live longer and healthier lives.
5 Leonardo da Vinci was an artist and also a brilliant ____________ (**invent**).
6 For every problem, there is usually a ____________ (**solve**).

4 Choose the correct word to complete the sentences.

1 Who **discovered / invented** America, Christopher Columbus or Leif Ericson?
2 Thomas Edison **discovered / invented** the electric light bulb in 1879.
3 Claudia spends a lot of time in the library doing **investigation / research** for her school projects.
4 The police conducted a thorough **investigation / research** after the theft.
5 The great thing about laptops is that they are **mobile / portable**.
6 My father keeps all his gardening **tools / appliances** in the garage.

Reading 2: vocabulary

1 Use a word or phrase from the box in each gap to complete the sentences.

figured out • gradually • brainwave • debt • sealed • emigrate

1 When you owe money to people or banks, you are in ____________ .
2 If you have a really wonderful new idea, it's called a ____________ .
3 When people leave their own country and move to another they ____________ .
4 If you have ____________ the solution to a problem, you have found the solution.
5 When something is closed so tightly that no air gets in or out, it is ____________ .
6 If you do something slowly or step by step, you do it ____________ .

E Use of English: exam practice

Read the text below and decide which answer (A, B, C or D) best fits each gap.

ALFRED NOBEL

When we hear the name Nobel, we immediately think of the Nobel Prizes. But Alfred Nobel, the (1) ______________ of the awards, was also a great scientist and inventor.

Born in 1833 in Sweden, Nobel studied first in Russia and then (2) ______________ to the US, where he studied mechanical (3) ______________ . Afterwards, he returned to Sweden to work with his father. Gradually, they made (4) ______________ in explosives. Nobel (5) ______________ out how to work safely with nitroglycerine, a very dangerous and explosive (6) ______________ . His invention later became known (7) ______________ dynamite. Nobel continued throughout his life to (8) ______________ improvements in the field of explosives.

He eventually owned (9) ______________ explosives factories around the world and became very wealthy.

Alfred Nobel was a man of great (10) ______________ . When he died he left a wonderful gift to the world: the Nobel Prizes. Each year these prizes are (11) ______________ to scientists, inventors and other creative people for their great (12) ______________ to the world.

	A	B	C	D
1	**A** holder	**B** creator	**C** discoverer	**D** receiver
2	**A** transferred	**B** visited	**C** joined	**D** emigrated
3	**A** developing	**B** producing	**C** engineering	**D** creating
4	**A** directions	**B** advances	**C** motions	**D** movements
5	**A** figured	**B** solved	**C** granted	**D** introduced
6	**A** shape	**B** form	**C** body	**D** substance
7	**A** by	**B** with	**C** as	**D** for
8	**A** do	**B** have	**C** make	**D** take
9	**A** numerous	**B** numerate	**C** numerical	**D** numbered
10	**A** advantage	**B** achievement	**C** situation	**D** incident
11	**A** awarded	**B** designed	**C** suggested	**D** implanted
12	**A** involvement	**B** contribution	**C** manufacturing	**D** development

G Grammar 2

1 Use *a*, *an* or *the* in each gap to complete the text. If no article is required, use a dash (–).

Michael's father is (1) ____ president of (2) ____ large computer science research company. He started (3) ____ company twenty-five years ago when he had just finished (4) ____ college. His company develops (5) ____ technology for (6) ____ defence industry and even for (7) ____ government! They also investigate new ways to use new technology in everyday life. That sounds like (8) ____ perfect job for me! I'd be (9) ____ great researcher and I love to work with (10) ____ computers.

2 There are eight mistakes with articles in the text on the right. Find the mistakes.

TEENAGE CLICKS

As the teenagers are particularly open to a new technology, companies that target this market are being advised to use the internet not only as a way to communicate their message to teens, but also to hear back from them. For an instance, a recent consumer survey of teenagers' online behaviour conducted by the global research firm Jupiter MMXI emphasises how the teenagers are 'spreading the word'. Almost a forty per cent said that they shared an information they had found on the net several times a week. Indeed, the primary reason most teenagers log on is to communicate with the people of their age group. Throughout the Europe, chat and email services feature among the most popular online destinations.

3 Choose the correct word or phrase to complete the sentences.

1. I'll repair my laptop as soon as I **will know / know** what's wrong with it!
2. Can I have your old mobile phone after you **bought / buy** a new one?
3. Be sure to turn off your computer before you **are leave/ leaving**.
4. I'll see you later tonight when the science club meeting **ends / will end**.
5. I'll call you while **I'll go / I'm going** home on the bus.
6. Sarah wants to be a computer programmer when she **will grow / grows** up.
7. Molly's going to lend me her new CD after she **will listen / has listened** to it.

E Use of English: exam practice

1 Read the text below. Use the word given in capitals at the end of some of the lines to form a word that fits in the gap in the same line. Write your answers IN CAPITAL LETTERS.

FAMOUS ME!

I sometimes wish I were a great (1) ________________ like Edison or Marconi. My name	**INVENT**
would go down in history for having (2) ________________ something totally new. You can	**DISCOVER**
really change people's lives if you come up with something (3) ________________ . Perhaps	**REVOLUTION**
I would also be famous for being extremely (4) ________________ with technology. I would	**CREATE**
be the most famous and respected (5) ________________ in the world! What a great brain I	**SCIENCE**
would have! I wouldn't just restrict myself to science, though. What about maths? I would find	
(6) ________________ to the most difficult mathematical equations. I would be responsible for	**SOLVE**
new (7) ________________ that would change the way people work and play. Doing something	**PRODUCE**
important like that would be (8) ________________ to people the whole world over, rich or poor.	**BENEFIT**
Everyone would know about my latest technological (9) ________________ and would thank	**DEVELOP**
me for the many great (10) ________________ of my life! Yes, that would suit me fine!	**ACHIEVE**

2 Complete the second sentence so that it has a similar meaning to the first sentence, using the word given. Do not change the word given. You must use between two and five words, including the word given. Write the missing words IN CAPITAL LETTERS.

1 If your computer stops working properly, you should call a technician.
down
If your computer ________________, you should call a technician.

2 I don't understand this physics homework.
figure
I can't ________________ do this physics homework.

3 We often don't think about how much technology helps us in our daily lives.
granted
We ________________ how much technology helps our daily lives.

4 You shouldn't turn off your computer until you have closed all the programs.
before
Close all the programs ________________ your computer.

5 She'll return on Monday and she'll contact you right away.
as
She'll contact you ________________ back on Monday.

6 I'll be working in the laboratory until seven, so call me before then.
while
Call me ________________ in the laboratory.

7 Have you discovered who invented safety pins?
found
Have you ________________ of safety pins was?

8 It would be great if someone discovered a way to travel through time!
come
Someone should ________________ a way to travel through time!

E Listening: exam practice

CD Track 3 You will hear five different people talking about problems with technology. For questions 1–5, choose from the list (A–F) the problem each speaker had. Use the letters only once. There is one extra letter which you do not need to use.

A	I didn't read the instructions.	Speaker 1	____
B	I bought one that was poor quality.	Speaker 2	____
C	I was embarrassed to use it.	Speaker 3	____
D	I lost an important part.	Speaker 4	____
E	I found it too complicated.	Speaker 5	____
F	I got the wrong advice.		

4

Money

Reading 1: vocabulary

1 Use a word from the box in each gap to complete the phrases.

invest • for • fortune • business • poverty • well

1 to be ______________ off
2 to live in ______________
3 to make a ______________
4 to ______________ money
5 to go ______________ it
6 to go into ______________

2 Match phrases from exercise 1 to these definitions.

a to try to achieve something ______________
b to be rich ______________
c to become rich ______________
d to be poor ______________
e to start a company ______________
f to put your money into a business in order to make more ______________

3 Choose the correct word or phrase to complete the sentences.

1 You have to have **dedication / company** if you want to succeed in business.
2 When James was ready to buy the bike, he took all his **fortune / savings** out of the bank.
3 Her business didn't make any money because she didn't have enough **clients / entrepreneurs**.
4 They didn't sell many games because they weren't **badly off / cheap** enough.
5 His father **does / makes** about €200,000 a year.
6 You need a lot of skills and abilities to **run / hold** a business successfully.
7 You will never sell anything unless there is a **partner / market** for it.
8 By becoming a millionaire at 19 years old, he **achieved / succeeded** what thousands of teenagers would like to do.

Grammar 1

1 Match to make sentences.

1 If you learn to manage money when you are young, ____
2 If I were you, ____
3 I'll take an extra €20 in case ____
4 If you're finding it hard to get by, ____
5 If you had enough money, ____
6 I'll give you this €100 as long as ____

a I would put my money in the bank where it is safe.
b you promise to pay me back next month.
c it's a habit that stays with you for life.
d try not to go out so much at weekends.
e I see something I want to buy.
f would you buy a new CD player?

2 Choose the correct word or phrase to complete the sentences.

1 You'll never be rich ______________________ you start saving money now.
a provided **b** unless **c** as long as

2 If you ______________________ me the list, I'll pick up your shopping for you.
a gave **b** will give **c** give

3 If I knew where the money was, I ______________________ tell you.
a will **b** would **c** can

4 Take an extra €5 ______________________ case it has gone up in price.
a the **b** if **c** in

5 I'll pay for your ticket this week, as long ______________________ you pay for me next time.
a as **b** time **c** that

6 If you need more money, ______________________ me and I'll send some.
a will call **b** to call **c** call

3 If a sentence is correct, put a tick (✔). If it is incorrect, rewrite it correctly.

1 If you do not have any money, life is difficult.
2 If you go to the office, the bank manager will speak to you.
3 If you will have financial problems, get some advice.
4 If I were you, I don't buy that car.
5 If I can buy anything I want, I would buy a house in the country.
6 If I need money, I ask my parents.
7 I can't afford to go to the cinema tonight except Mum gives me some money.
8 Helen took her purse in case that the bank was closed.
9 I'll buy it for you as long you promise to use it.
10 You can't buy a motorbike unless you are over 17.

E Use of English: exam practice

Read the text below and think of the word which best fits each gap. Use only one word in each gap. Write your answers IN CAPITAL LETTERS.

There are a number of things any young entrepreneur should consider before setting (1) ______________ a business. The first, naturally, is where you are going to get the capital. (2) ______________ you are lucky enough to have (3) ______________ into some money early in life, that means you are going to have to (4) ______________ it, probably from a bank. You will have (5) ______________ chance of getting a loan from a bank (6) ______________ you don't have a well-organised business plan. Provided (7) ______________ you can show you have a market for your new business, though, you stand a good chance of getting a bank to invest (8) ______________ it. In the beginning, things might be difficult but (9) ______________ to be patient. Rome wasn't built in a day. You might have to do (10) ______________ some luxuries in life until you build up the business. It's also a good idea to put some money aside in (11) ______________ of an emergency. Many businesses have (12) ______________ down because the people running them didn't plan ahead for rough patches.

E Reading: exam practice

You are going to read a magazine article about what young people think about the world and their futures. For questions 1–15, choose from the people (A–E). The people may be chosen more than once.

Which person

thinks many young people exaggerate how hard life is? 1 ___
says young people sometimes act before they think? 2 ___
knows what they want to do and how to achieve it? 3 ___
believes young people should pay more attention to politics? 4 ___
would like today's young people to manage the world better than other generations? 5 ___
believes the world's wealth isn't handled correctly? 6 ___
thinks young people are obsessed with wealth? 7 ___
resents the fact that young people today have fewer chances than in the past? 8 ___
says that the world can only be changed by making an effort? 9 ___
prefers the modern world to other eras? 10 ___
thinks the older generation are scared of original ideas? 11 ___
believes young people don't realise how hard it is to be successful? 12 ___
says getting a good education means accepting you will have to borrow lots of money? 13 ___
thinks the government doesn't do enough to help the poor? 14 ___
believes the world is improving at a steady pace? 15 ___

OUR WORLD?

A Bethany Wilkins

It seems to me that the people who have been left in charge of our economies have no idea how to solve the problems the world has. I really don't understand how so much money can be wasted. Even in the developed world there's a massive difference between the richest and the poorest. This tells me that the world's resources are being very poorly managed. I think the problem is that politicians are stuck in their ways and are afraid to try anything new in case it frightens voters. Sometimes, I think that older people have too much experience of the world and that doesn't help them to come up with fresh ideas. Young people can be impulsive but I think they are much more creative thinkers.

B Josh Haines

Sometimes I feel very angry and bitter about the world my generation is going to inherit. There are so few real opportunities for young people these days. Most of the available jobs are poorly paid and there's a lot of competition for decent jobs. If you want to get a good job through a higher education, you have to be prepared to get into a lot of debt that will take years to repay. But I try not to feel too down because I think that if you have the will to succeed then you will find a way. I hope my generation do a better job of making the world a decent place for the future.

C Daniel Pierce

A lot of young people I know are always talking about how awful everything in the world is. I really don't understand what they mean, especially for us in the developed world. Provided that you're not one of the small number of people who are extremely poor, then you probably have a very decent life. I think people just like to complain. They notice negative things but don't notice the positive ones. The world is definitely becoming a better place – it's happening slowly but surely. I'm certainly glad I live in the modern world we have now and wouldn't want to live in any past age. I think that life will get even better in the future, too, thanks to technology.

D Lucy Craig

The government should definitely do more to help those at the bottom of the ladder in society. There is no doubt that there is too much inequality. But I think that my future is mainly in my own hands. I'm determined to do well in my life and I've got many plans and ambitions for the future. A lot of my peer group expect things to be handed to them on a plate. They think the world owes them a living. I think it's up to everyone to be responsible for their own lives. It's up to us to change the world and that won't happen if we're sitting at home playing on a games console, waiting for opportunity to knock on our door. It won't.

E Ainsley Dawson

Most people my age don't care about what's happening around them. As long as they're OK then they're not interested in anything else. I think we should be interested in politics and what's happening in the world. It's our duty as citizens of the world. Basically, my generation is too spoilt and has had it too easy to care. They think poverty is something that happens to people in faraway places and that they have an easy life to look forward to. They're only interested in being rich or famous and think that money is the solution to everything. They also want to have plenty of money without really working for it. I think many of them are naive and irresponsible.

V Vocabulary

1 Choose the correct word to complete the sentences.

1 Can I **lend / borrow** your pen, please?
2 I'll **lend / borrow** you the money, as long as you pay me back tomorrow.
3 The tourist **company / industry** is very important for Greece.
4 Many people lost their jobs in the **economic / economical** crisis.
5 It's often more **economic / economical** to buy one large packet than two small packets.

2 Use a word or phrase from the box in each gap to complete the sentences.

checkout • refund • cheques • bargains • discount cashpoint • change • receipt • credit card • currency

1 'Do you know there's a 50% ______________ on all women's clothes at Stephanie's Store this week?'
'50%? Quick! Where's my ______________ ? We're going right now to pick up some ______________ !'
2 'Can I pay in any ______________ I want to – for example, dollars?'
'No, Madam. I'm sorry but ______________ can only be accepted in euros.'
3 'Oh, no! We can't go to the ______________ . I don't think we've got enough money for all this shopping!'
'Don't worry. There's a ______________ over there. I'll go and get some money while you wait in the queue.'
4 'Did you go back to the shop and get a ______________ for that CD that you bought which didn't play?'
'No. I couldn't find the ______________ . I looked everywhere. I think I was so busy checking the ______________ that I forgot to pick it up.'

3 Use one word in each gap to complete the sentences.

1 I've been saving ______________ all winter and now I'm going to take a long holiday.
2 I don't think I like that dress I bought. I think I'll take it ______________ to the shop and see if they'll change it for me.
3 Some people in this country have so little money that they struggle to get ______________ .
4 When her aunt died, she came ______________ a fortune and never had to work another day in her life.
5 After leaving school, he set ______________ his own business writing computer programs.
6 When my grandparents were younger, they often had to do ______________ fresh fruit because there was none in the shops.

E Use of English: exam practice

Read the text below. Use the word given in capitals at the end of some of the lines to form a word that fits in the gap in the same line. Write your answers IN CAPITAL LETTERS.

TARGETING THE TEENAGE INVESTOR

Traditionally, banks have aimed their (1) ______________ at those with plenty of money.	**ADVERTISE**
(2) ______________ however, banks today are trying to attract younger and younger	**INCREASE**
(3) ______________ – people like you! The idea behind it is that if they can get you young	**CONSUME**
enough, they will be able to depend on your (4) ______________ for the rest of your life. And	**LOYAL**
there is so much (5) ______________ between the different banks that they will try almost	**COMPETE**
anything to get their hands on your (6) ______________ . So be prepared for their free offers.	**SAVE**
They will tempt you with anything from holidays to (7) ______________ items of clothing.	**FASHION**
One high street bank is even offering a (8) ______________ stereo system to all first-time	**STYLE**
customers. That's not a bad return on your (9) ______________ ! And there's another good	**INVEST**
reason to put your money in the bank – free (10) ______________ advice. You never know	**FINANCE**
when you might need that!	

Reading 2: vocabulary

1 **Use a word from the box in each gap to complete the sentences.**

hygiene • demands • see • influence • possess • well-being

1 I was quite shocked when I found out that a very small number of people in the country ______________ the great majority of the wealth.
2 Once you understand the purpose of advertising, you begin to ______________ through the tricks they use to persuade you to buy things.
3 Anywhere where food is being prepared, such as a restaurant, good ______________ is extremely important.
4 As the hotel manager, you'll be responsible for the day-to-day running of the hotel and the ______________ of the guests.
5 I finally decided that I had had enough of the ______________ of such a difficult career and I left my job.
6 It might not always seem fair, but it's a fact of life that rich people have more ______________ than the rest of us.

2 **Choose the correct word to complete the text.**

If they were left to themselves, advertising (1) **agencies / offices** would be tempted to make claims for products that weren't true. In order to protect (2) **grown-ups / consumers**, most countries control advertising in some way. Usually, there are (3) **influences / regulations** about what you can and can't say about a product, and the authorities have the power to impose a (4) **ban / stop** on certain advertisements. For example, you might be able to imply that a certain product increases your social (5) **level / status**, but you can't say that it will give you a healthier (6) **living / lifestyle** without some kind of proof.

G Grammar 2

1 Use a word from the box in each gap to complete the sentences.

a • some • much • many • few • little

1 Only a ______________ of my friends get more pocket money than I do.
2 He went to the bank manager to get ______________ advice about his business.
3 I have got very ______________ money left after the weekend.
4 David didn't have ______________ money so he went to the library instead of the CD shop.
5 I have ______________ little money. Shall we go for a cup of coffee?
6 I don't have ______________ friends who earn their own money.

2 If a sentence is correct, put a tick (✔). If it is incorrect, rewrite it correctly.

1 I feel that I am lucky because I have few friends who would lend me money if I needed it.
2 There are not many furnitures in my room because I can't afford to buy things I like.
3 I went shopping this morning and bought a new trouser.
4 You need to buy a wood to fix that table.
5 I haven't read the news for ages, so if you're passing the newsagent's, can you get me a paper?
6 I wonder if you could give me some advices about what MP3 player to buy?

E Use of English: exam practice

1 Read the text below and decide which answer (A, B, C or D) best fits each gap.

DECORATING A TEENAGER'S BEDROOM

In the past, the children of the household had very (1) ______________ choice in the way their bedrooms were decorated. The fact that families had many (2) ______________ children than they do now was an important consideration. This meant that there was not (3) ______________ money available to pay for more than the basics – paint or wallpaper. Add to this the fact that children of differing ages – and tastes – had to share a room and it is easy to see why, when it (4) ______________ to decorating, not much thought was put into the job. Times change, however, and now the amount spent on home decorating and DIY is (5) ______________ at over €8 billion a year. Families have acquired greater spending power and children have more of a voice; in other words, parents have to take notice (6) ______________ what they want. What has become very clear is that most teenagers are aware of the latest (7) ______________ and they really do have a very good idea of the way they want their personal space decorated. It is then up to their parents to help them achieve the look they want. Money is still going to be a consideration – (8) ______________, of course, you have recently come into a fortune. But there is a wide range of materials to choose from and it really does pay to (9) ______________ around. There are (10) ______________ available throughout the year, so it can be done quite (11) ______________. Parents may argue that their child's choices are not appropriate, but it is the teenager who has to live with it, not them. After all, if the teenager (12) ______________ for a colour or a material that the parent considers impractical, this can always be discussed!

	A	B	C	D
1	**A** little	**B** few	**C** poor	**D** some
2	**A** extra	**B** more	**C** lots	**D** of
3	**A** any	**B** much	**C** more	**D** some
4	**A** went	**B** said	**C** became	**D** came
5	**A** claimed	**B** estimated	**C** guessed	**D** considered
6	**A** of	**B** to	**C** about	**D** from
7	**A** models	**B** news	**C** sales	**D** trends
8	**A** and	**B** but	**C** unless	**D** if
9	**A** buy	**B** study	**C** sell	**D** shop
10	**A** purchases	**B** incomes	**C** markets	**D** bargains
11	**A** economically	**B** financially	**C** commercially	**D** profitably
12	**A** chooses	**B** goes	**C** thinks	**D** decides

2 **Complete the second sentence so that it has a similar meaning to the first sentence, using the word given. Do not change the word given. You must use between two and five words, including the word given. Write the missing words IN CAPITAL LETTERS.**

1 There aren't many notes left in my wallet. **only**

There ______________________ notes left in my wallet.

2 Paul started work at six o'clock this morning and he still hasn't come home. **working**

Paul ______________________ six o'clock this morning and he still hasn't come home.

3 Did you manage to persuade George to lend you some money? **succeed**

Did you ______________________ George to lend you some money?

4 Unless we leave soon, we won't get to the bank before it closes. **if**

We won't get to the bank before it closes ______________________ leave soon.

5 Could you lend me some money? **borrow**

Could ______________________ you?

6 I'll take the job provided that the salary's high enough. **long**

I'll take the job ______________________ the salary's high enough.

7 How did they find the money to buy such an expensive car? **up**

How did they ______________________ the money to buy such an expensive car?

8 I've got little money to spend on luxuries at the moment. **a**

I ______________________ of money to spend on luxuries at the moment.

E Listening: exam practice

CD Track 4 You will hear an interview with a financial expert. For questions 1–5, choose the best answer (A, B or C).

1 Most of the people who see Tessa have a problem with
A borrowing too much. **B** understanding their bank account. **C** paying their household bills.

2 Using a credit card often makes people
A buy things they don't want. **B** spend more than they should. **C** ignore the prices of things.

3 The first thing people with large credit card bills should do is
A call their bank manager. **B** get advice from an expert. **C** contact their credit card company.

4 Tessa advises people with financial problems to
A destroy their credit cards. **B** use their credit cards carefully. **C** lock their credit cards away.

5 Some of the people that see Tessa
A think she's wrong about credit cards. **B** realise that they don't want a credit card.
C make the same mistakes again later.

5

Leisure

Reading 1: vocabulary

1 Match each word 1–8 with a meaning a–h.

1 addiction	___	**a** absolutely necessary
2 negotiation	___	**b** a set of rules or advice
3 essential	___	**c** mad, crazy
4 antidote	___	**d** forming a close relationship
5 guidelines	___	**e** strong desire / need for something
6 bonding	___	**f** get in the way of
7 hamper	___	**g** solution, alternative
8 berserk	___	**h** discussion to reach an agreement

2 Use a word from the box in the correct form in each gap to complete the sentences.

nag • exasperate • spend • miss • keep

1 He ______________ most of his time last weekend playing with his smartphone.
2 I can't stand it! She's always ______________ me about something.
3 I'm afraid you ______________ out on a great party last week when you were away.
4 The online news site ______________ me up to date with current affairs.
5 She is the most ______________ person I've ever met!

Grammar 1

1 Choose the correct word or phrase to complete the sentences.

1 You **ought / should** to come to the concert tonight. It's going to be fabulous!
2 Please **must / may** I come with you to the game this Saturday?
3 Ryan **could / should** have had a party if he had asked his parents.
4 Nicole **couldn't / shouldn't** go out in the evening until she was fifteen.
5 Do you **have to / must** play your music so loud? It's driving me crazy!
6 Jerry **must / ought to** have joined the drama club. He would have enjoyed it.

2 Decide what the function of the modal is in the sentences. Write A for ability, O for obligation, C for criticism, AD for advice and P for permission.

1 You **shouldn't** read so much in the dark. You'll hurt your eyes. _____
2 Larry **has to** go on a family picnic this Saturday. _____
3 If I do my homework first, **can** I go with my friends to the cinema on Thursday? _____

4 You **ought to** have phoned when you realised you were going to be late. ____
5 When I was young I **could** speak Italian rather well. ____
6 **Can** you help me figure out how to set up this exercise equipment? ____

3 Use a word or phrase from the box in each gap to complete the sentences.

should have • don't have to • can't • mustn't • should • had to

1 Beth __________ queue up for hours to buy tickets for Saturday's concert.
2 My little brother __________ understand why he's not allowed to play on his own outside after dark.
3 We __________ got seats in the front row. I can't see the stage from here.
4 You __________ play your music so loud! It disturbs the neighbours.
5 You __________ come to Grandma's with us, but she'd really be happy if you did.
6 Do you think I __________ dye my hair before the ball next week?

E Use of English: exam practice

Complete the second sentence so that it has a similar meaning to the first sentence, using the word given. Do not change the word given. You must use between two and five words, including the word given. Write the missing words IN CAPITAL LETTERS.

1 There was no reason for Mary to storm off like she did.
have
Mary __________ storm off like that.

2 Our headteacher gave us permission to have a school ball!
said
Our headteacher __________ a school ball!

3 Children under sixteen are not allowed in the nightclub.
get
You __________ the nightclub if you're under sixteen.

4 Be more careful next time and you won't get hurt again.
will
You __________ more careful if you don't want to get hurt next time.

5 I am absolutely incapable of speaking French without an accent.
speak
I simply __________ French without an accent.

6 It isn't necessary to ask Jacob to the party, but I think he'd like to come.
not
You __________ Jacob to the party, but I think he'd like to come.

7 I wish I could go to a fashion show in Paris!
able
I'd love __________ go to a fashion show in Paris!

8 Why didn't you tell Rod what time we were meeting?
should
You __________ Rod what time we were meeting.

E Reading: exam practice

You are going to read an article about teenagers and free time. Seven sentences have been removed from the article. Choose from the sentences A–H the one which fits each gap (1–7). There is one extra sentence which you do not need to use.

A When they can afford the trip, they love to travel to other cities to show their support at away games.

B In fact, almost all of their time away from school is spent doing homework and taking lessons.

C Away from the books, they try to make sure they take time out for a little fun and entertainment.

D While some might want to get away from all the activity, he says it suits him perfectly.

E It's a time to recharge the batteries and think things through.

F It might not sound very organised, but they wouldn't have it any other way.

G It's tough to keep up with it all, and the pressure is beginning to show.

H Most days, you'll find him working on his website or chatting to friends online.

Time Out

Andi Phillips interviewed a number of teenagers to find out just what they're up to when they're out having fun.

School's over, the homework's done and you've finished any household chores you have to do. What do you do when it's entirely up to you? How do you fill your free time? It seems that teenagers have a thousand and one things that they like to do, from hobbies to sports, from reading to playing music. The young people I spoke to all had interesting things to tell me about what today's teens like to do.

Jemma and Julie are twins, both 16 last month. They're good students at school and spend a lot of time studying. [1] That usually means that a free afternoon or evening for these girls is spent at the cinema with friends. 'I'm crazy about action movies,' says Jemma. 'They're just so exciting!' Julie agrees and explains that going to the cinema is almost an addiction for them. 'If I don't see at least one movie at the weekend, I really feel I've missed something great.'

Charlie is 15 years old and has his own ideas on how to spend his leisure time. 2 At the weekend, though, he abandons the world of technology in favour of his other hobby – bowling! Charlie's favourite way to unwind is to bowl for a few hours at the local bowling alley. 'We've got a nice league going, and it's great fun. Bowling lets you escape from the pressures of school and just enjoy yourself for a while. It's great!'

Sean is 17 and his cousin Roger is 16. They both believe there's only one proper leisure activity – sport! In particular, football. Sean and Roger are both players and fans. They play for the school team and attend as many of their local team's games as they can. 3 Faces painted in team colours, Sean and Roger are sure to be the ones jumping up and down in front of the camera when their team scores. 'There's nothing more exciting than sport,' says Sean. Roger adds that being a player goes hand in hand with being a fan of a professional team. 'I can't imagine being one and not the other.'

Valerie and Sue are both 17 and are not very specific about what they do in their free time, probably because they don't actually have any hobbies! They go window shopping, maybe sit for a drink or a quick bite to eat somewhere, and in general, just 'hang out'. 4 'It's hard to say exactly what we do when we hang out, but it's important that we get together whenever we can. We're such good friends that we have loads of fun even if we're just sitting in a fast-food restaurant talking!'

Fifteen-year-old Monica and her brother Freddy, 14, say that they don't have much leisure time at all. 5 'It might sound sad, but in my free time I usually do something like practise the piano. I don't mind because I'm getting really good. One day I'll be glad I put in the time to learn.' Freddy agrees and adds, 'You don't have to be fooling around or getting into trouble to have fun. I'm taking karate lessons on Saturdays with two of my schoolmates and we have a great time!'

Simon is 15 and comes from a very large family. With six brothers and sisters and 24 cousins, there are an awful lot of people around the house to spend time with. 6 'I'd say most of my leisure time is spent with my family, just doing different things together. There are so many of us coming and going from each other's houses all the time, it's like we're always having a party,' Simon says. 'Sure, my friends come round and we hang out sometimes, but usually I'm doing something with someone from my family. We're all really close to each other.'

Judith admits she's a bit of a loner, and says she likes to have some time to herself everyday. 7 'I see my friends often enough,' she says, 'but I really need time alone, although it's not always easy to find the time to get away.' When no-one's around Judith likes to read or listen to music. She finds being alone very relaxing. When asked if she gets lonely, she's very quick to point out that being alone is not the same at all as being lonely.

V Vocabulary

1 Use a word from the box in each gap to complete the sentences.

cast • audience • spectator • lifeguard • host • crowd

1 I'm not much of an athlete, but I love to watch sports. I'm a great ______________.
2 After the performance, the director held a party for the ______________ to thank them for their hard work.
3 My favourite talk show ______________ is Mario on *Mario Live*. He's the greatest!
4 Michael got a summer job as a ______________ at the beach.
5 When our team won the championship, the ______________ went absolutely wild!
6 Have you ever been part of a live TV ______________? It's really exciting.

2 Choose the correct word or phrase to complete the sentences.

1 In-line skating really **came across / caught on** a few years back.
2 Why don't you **come across / come round** to my place for lunch on Saturday?
3 Here, **flick through / take up** this magazine for a minute and tell me if you like it.
4 Mara would really like to **take up / take to** yoga this year.
5 I've tried yoga before, but I didn't **take up / take to** it right away.
6 I'll meet you at 5.30 if I can **come across / get away** from work early.

3 Use a form of the words in brackets in each gap to complete the sentences.

1 There is always a lot of ____________________ (**active**) in the park on Sunday.
2 I found the play very ____________________ (**amuse**). Did you enjoy it?
3 The audience showed their ____________________ (**appreciate**) with loud applause.
4 ____________________ (**attend**) was at an all time high at last night's match.
5 I find painting with watercolours more ____________________ (**enjoy**) than oils.
6 The ____________________ (**enter**) to the theatre was hidden by the large crowd.
7 My favourite form of ____________________ (**entertain**) is listening to music.
8 There's so much ____________________ (**excite**) about next weekend's ball.

4 Choose the correct word or phrase to complete the sentences.

1 How did you manage **getting / to get** free tickets to the ball?
2 Julie finally succeeded **in persuading / to persuade** her parents to let her have flying lessons.
3 Jane was able **to organise / of organising** another very popular programme of social events this year.
4 I've arranged **to meet / meeting** Jerry after chess club tonight.
5 My brother really enjoys **to play / playing** squash.
6 My parents never allowed me **wearing / to wear** make-up before I was fifteen.
7 Does your mum let you **to go / go** out on week nights?

Reading 2: vocabulary

1 Use a word from the box to replace the word or phrase in bold.

notion • reasonable • twist • obstacles • current • cable

1 An athlete has to overcome many **difficulties** before he can succeed. ______________
2 If you **turn** your neck around like this, you can almost see the sea from this window. ______________
3 I think the prices at that new sports shop are **not too expensive**. ______________
4 The **idea** that we all have loads of free time is just ridiculous! ______________
5 The ski lift runs on a thick steel **wire** all the way up the mountain. ______________
6 You don't even have to swim in the water park. The **water flow** just pulls you along! ______________

Grammar 2

1 Choose the correct word to complete the sentences.

1 That was the **more / most** exciting ride I have ever been on!
2 Mix Master is definitely better **than / from** any other DJ on the radio today.
3 We have the **bigger / biggest** football stadium in the area.
4 I've never seen a **worse / worst** movie than this one!
5 It was nowhere near as **good / better** as the book.
6 She acted more **dramatically / dramatic** than she has in any of her other films.

2 Use a form of the words in brackets in each gap to complete the sentences.

1 That was the ______________ (**expensive**) holiday we have ever been on.
2 My second year of secondary school was much ______________ (**good**) than the first year.
3 I didn't like maths much, but physics was my ______________ (**less**) favourite subject!
4 This book is ______________ (**long**) than the others in the series but much ______________ (**interesting**). I love the plot!
5 It was a lot ______________ (**difficult**) to get my mum to let me wear make-up than I had thought.
6 *Celebrity Surprise* is by far the ______________ (**funny**) programme I've seen this year.

3 Use the correct form of the words in brackets to complete the questions.

1 ______________ (**you / see**) the newest kung fu movie yet? I hear it's excellent.
2 ______________ (**you / be**) busy yesterday afternoon, because I didn't see you after school?
3 What ______________ (**Sam / do**) with the CDs I lent him? He can't find them now!
4 Who ______________ (**decorate**) the hall for the dance? It looks great.
5 Why ______________ (**you / not / call**) me yesterday? I wanted to talk to you.
6 Who ______________ (**Sean / invite**) to the dance next week? Has he decided yet?

4 **Circle the correct word or phrase to complete the text.**

Hi Sue!

I have to tell you about the (1) **more / most** fantastic holiday (2) **that / than** I've ever been on. It was a combination of camping and a canoe trip. (3) **Have / Did** you ever done anything like that before? I hadn't! It was more frightening (4) **as / than** I'd imagined it would be. The rapids feel (5) **much / many** more dangerous when you're actually on the river (6) **from / than** they seem on the river bank. And the waterfalls had really (7) **steep / steeper** drops! Although it was a bit scary, I have to say that it was totally exhilarating! The camping part was also great fun, but not as exciting (8) **as / than** the canoe trip. It was definitely the (9) **most of / most** relaxing part of the whole trip. (10) **Most / The most** of the people on the trip said they're going again next year. I know I am! And who (11) **you / do you** think I want to come with me? You! Would (12) **you / do you** like to?

E Use of English: exam practice

1 **Read the text below and decide which answer (A, B, C or D) best fits each gap.**

The Circus

Everybody loves the circus. For almost 300 years, across Europe, Russia and America, 'children of all ages' have been (1) __________ by the animals and acrobats of the circus. The first circus was founded in England in 1769 by Philip Astley, who performed horse-riding stunts for a small (2) __________. He then travelled throughout Europe and established circuses in many other countries. The circuses usually took place in outdoor areas in a circle or a ring surrounded by (3) __________. The performers (4) __________ their audiences with exciting acrobatic acts and horse-riding (5) __________. Circuses as we know them today are (6) __________ displays – sometimes with several tents – of wild animals and remarkable acrobatics. The facilities consist of tents with shows taking place at the same time, the (7) __________ both amusing and (8) __________ their audiences. Some of the most (9) __________ circuses in history which continue to be extremely (10) __________ today include the American Barnum & Bailey Ringling Brothers Circus, which (11) __________ itself 'The Greatest Show on Earth', the Canadian Cirque du Soleil, the Moscow Circus and Billy Smart's Circus of London. Millions of people (12) __________ them around the world each year.

	A	B	C	D
1	**A** appealed	**B** enjoyed	**C** laughed	**D** entertained
2	**A** viewer	**B** guest	**C** cast	**D** audience
3	**A** crowds	**B** hosts	**C** characters	**D** spectators
4	**A** informed	**B** thrilled	**C** concerned	**D** kicked
5	**A** performances	**B** plays	**C** stages	**D** theatres
6	**A** infinite	**B** eternal	**C** massive	**D** awful
7	**A** guests	**B** performers	**C** athletes	**D** producers
8	**A** acting	**B** talking	**C** frightening	**D** showing
9	**A** known	**B** infamous	**C** notorious	**D** famous
10	**A** popular	**B** accepted	**C** common	**D** regular
11	**A** says	**B** calls	**C** names	**D** tells
12	**A** go	**B** stay	**C** attend	**D** take

2 **Read the text below and think of the word which best fits each gap. Use only one word in each gap. Write your answers IN CAPITAL LETTERS.**

American County Fairs

Each summer, counties all (1) ______________ the United States hold county fairs. The fairs have been taking place for more (2) ______________ 150 years, and serve as a good way to bring (3) ______________ people of the county together for a little food and fun. Typically, a county fair has a variety (4) ______________ activities and events. Central to every fair, however, (5) ______________ the animal shows. Participants from tots to teens have the opportunity to prepare, then present, their animal for show. The shows are judged (6) ______________ experts, and one animal in every category wins a prize, usually a blue ribbon. The animals must (7) ______________ well fed, in good health and well groomed. Often the horses have bows and ribbons tied in their hair, and the rabbits wear fancy collars. The children take great pride in caring for their animals, and (8) ______________ forward to the fair every year.

Besides animals, there are also displays of handmade arts and crafts. These too are judged in competition with each (9) ______________. Looking at the handmade quilts and sweaters, one imagines what life was (10) ______________ a hundred years ago. The county fair competitions provide a good way (11) ______________ preserving old art forms for new generations. County fairs usually last (12) ______________ about a week, and are often held in July. Visitors like to make the trip to see the animals and crafts. Kids love the excitement too. All in all, a trip to the local county fair makes for a very pleasant summer's day.

E Listening: exam practice

CD Track 5 You will hear people talking in five different situations. For questions 1–5, choose the best answer (A, B or C).

1 You hear this boy talking on the phone. What is he going to do this weekend?
A play football **B** play pool **C** go bowling

2 You hear this woman talking about a night out. What did she dislike?
A the acting **B** the theatre **C** the costumes

3 You hear this man on the phone. What does he do?
A buy extra tickets for another date **B** change the date of his tickets
C change the seats on the tickets

4 You hear this woman talking. What did she think of the film?
A She thought it was too unrealistic. **B** She thought it was too romantic.
C She thought it was too complicated.

5 You hear this girl describing a video game. What did she particularly like about it?
A the graphics **B** the action **C** the music

6

Nature

Reading 1: vocabulary

1 Use a word from the box to complete the phrases.

population • trickle • developing • litter • extinct • processes • bank • conservation

1 a bottle ______________
2 a ______________ of water
3 the ______________ world
4 water ______________
5 the world's ______________
6 industrial ______________
7 to become ______________
8 to drop ______________

2 Choose the correct word or phrase.

1 Which of the following does *not* refer to rubbish in the street?
a litter **b** pick up **c** drop **d** leak

2 Which of the following does *not* refer to what people might do to protect the environment?
a protest **b** demonstrate **c** waste **d** take action

3 Which of the following does *not* refer to water?
a species **b** dams **c** reservoirs **d** sinks

4 Which of the following does *not* refer to animals?
a extinct **b** evaporation **c** endangered **d** wildlife

3 Use a word from the box in each gap to complete the sentences.

protesting • pollution • leaking • dam • evaporation • drought

1 ______________ pipes are responsible for the loss of thousands of tonnes of water every day.

2 There are plans to build a ______________ to stop the flow of the river and collect water in a reservoir.

3 ______________ from factories is one of the biggest problems facing our rivers and seas.

4 The recent ______________ in our country meant that there was not enough water and we all had to be very careful how much we used.

5 We should start ______________ against the trees being cut down in the nearby forest.

6 ______________ is when water disappears into the atmosphere.

Grammar 1

1 Use the correct passive tense to rewrite these sentences.

1 The cold weather has killed almost all the birds on the island.

____

2 We are encouraging people not to drop litter.

____

3 The local people have prevented the government from building a new reservoir.

____

4 Yesterday, they announced some dramatic news about the environment.

____

2 Use the prompts to write sentences in the passive.

1 the problem of noise pollution / study / government scientists at the moment
2 people / need / educate / about the benefits of recycling
3 a lot of water / can / save / turning the tap off when you are brushing your teeth
4 a demonstration / held / outside parliament yesterday to protest about air pollution
5 a documentary on endangered species / show / on TV at eight o'clock tonight
6 it / announce / a new kind of environmentally friendly petrol / produce / next year

3 Use a word from the box in each gap to complete the sentences.

being • been • be • are • was • have

1 After last month's fire, huge areas of forest __________ been destroyed.
2 Many old cars, fridges and cookers __________ simply dumped at the side of the road every year.
3 The situation regarding the polluted lake is __________ investigated by scientists.
4 The results of the study of insects will __________ released next month.
5 Government officials have __________ criticised for their plans to build the airport in an area of natural beauty.
6 A new law __________ introduced yesterday banning the use of a range of chemicals in industry.

4 Use a form of the verb in brackets in each gap to complete the text.

PROGRESS IN SAVING THE PLANET

Although over the last 20 years a great deal (1) __________ (**achieve**) in the protection and conservation of the environment, there is still an awful lot (2) __________ (**do**). According to some scientists, we (3) __________ (**manage**) to reduce the amount of damage we are doing to the atmosphere, and the hole in the ozone layer is starting to close. Thanks to dedicated individuals, species of plant and animal life which (4) __________ (**threaten**) with extinction have now (5) __________ (**save**). On the other hand, every day many species become extinct. Laws and regulations exist to stop factories polluting rivers and seas but this (6) __________ (**remain**) a major problem. And the use of cars means that we are still making our cities and towns unbearable to live in, despite the fact that progress (7) __________ (**make**) with public transport systems. So, while some problems (8) __________ (**solve**) already, we cannot afford to stop making an effort.

E Reading: exam practice

You are going to read an article from a website which is dedicated to ways of dealing with waste. For questions 1–8, choose the answer (A, B, C or D) which you think fits best according to the text.

1 The writer suggests that getting rid of old clothes can
- **A** benefit you and other people.
- **B** only be done through recycling bins.
- **C** cause a problem with rubbish.
- **D** save you time.

2 What does the writer say about buying clothes second-hand?
- **A** It is expensive and you can end up being a fashion victim.
- **B** All of today's top stars do it.
- **C** You save money, look different and it helps with recycling.
- **D** It is a fashionable thing to do but ordinary people can't afford it.

3 The Mailing Preference Service
- **A** keeps you informed about environmental issues.
- **B** collects paper from your home to be recycled.
- **C** provides your details to advertisers.
- **D** helps you to reduce the amount of rubbish you throw away.

www.rethinkrubbish.org

RETHINK RUBBISH @ HOME

Come on, admit it. We've all got clothes in our wardrobe that we haven't worn for years and we know we'll never wear again. Taking your old clothes to the local charity shop or recycling bin is a great way of getting rid of a load of rubbish and creating extra space at the same time! And it's all for a good cause. Charities such as The Salvation Army, Oxfam, TRAID and Scope are big collectors of old clothes, either through charity shops and recycling banks or for sorting and selling on, often abroad.

Buying second-hand clothes is now definitely in vogue too, with dedicated followers of fashion such as Kylie and Geri Halliwell leading the way. Vintage boutiques offer ranges of designer classics, but can be a bit on the expensive side, so why not raid your local charity shop to pick up a real bargain? You can create your own distinct look and feel good about your recycling effort.

Hate junk mail? Around one million tonnes of junk mail and magazines get binned each year! But it's easy to cut down on the rubbish in your bin by registering with the Mailing Preference Service. Send them your details and they'll make sure that you don't receive piles of unwanted offers and advertisements through your letterbox.

4 Many of the things we throw in our dustbins
  A come from the local supermarket.
  B can cause the bin to break.
  C are made of recycled material.
  D can easily be recycled.

5 What does the figure of £34 million represent?
  A The cost of recycling all the drinks cans in the UK.
  B The amount spent on soft drinks each year in the UK.
  C The annual cost of the aluminium used to make drinks cans.
  D The amount spent by supermarkets on recycling schemes.

6 The phrase 'time and time again' (line 23) suggests that
  A aluminium may be recycled more than once.
  B time is running out for the environment.
  C a huge number of cans are made every year.
  D the cans we use now will last forever.

7 What point does the writer make in the last paragraph?
  A Nobody tries to reduce the amount of rubbish they produce.
  B There are many ways to reduce the amount of rubbish we produce.
  C If we follow this advice, we will have no rubbish at all.
  D Our homes are too dirty because of all the rubbish.

8 This text is written for people who
  A are interested in producing less rubbish.
  B want to work in recycling.
  C can't afford to buy new products.
  D are thinking of donating to charity.

A massive 60% of the contents of your dustbin can be recycled. So why not give your bin a break and drop off your paper, card, glass bottles, jars and cans at the recycling banks located at most supermarkets? By doing this, you'll reduce your household waste by nearly one third!

Did you know that if you're really clever, there's £34 million worth of empty aluminium
drink cans in the UK just waiting to be collected and recycled? The reason is that
aluminium is really valuable and the sort that's made into the billions of drinks cans we
23 see on our supermarket shelves can be recycled and used time and time again to make
new drinks cans.

We produce over 26 million tonnes of household rubbish in the UK every year, so there's plenty of scope for us to Rethink Rubbish in the home! By thinking about the types of goods we buy, how we use them and where we dispose of them, we can dramatically reduce the amount of rubbish our homes produce. Whilst we can't get rid of rubbish altogether, there are hundreds of ways in which we can cut down on what we throw away. So, whether we're recycling, finding new uses for 'junk' or simply reducing what we create in the first place, with a little effort, we can all make our homes cleaner and greener!

V Vocabulary

1 Complete each phrasal verb.

1 to die ____________ (= to become extinct)
2 to go ____________ (= to stop being fresh)
3 to cut ____________ a tree
4 to run ____________ of something
5 to throw something ____________

2 Use the correct preposition in each gap to complete the phrases.

1 to refer ____________ something
2 to accuse somebody ____________ something
3 to depend ____________ somebody ____________ something
4 to take care ____________ something
5 to inform people ____________ something

3 Use a word from the box in each gap to complete the phrases.

effect • reserve • species • warming • fuels • system

1 sewerage ____________
2 endangered ____________
3 greenhouse ____________
4 global ____________
5 nature ____________
6 fossil ____________

4 Choose the correct word or phrase to complete the sentences.

1 After seven years in the city, he had had enough of **rural / urban** life.
2 One modern problem facing many of us is that of **fog / smog**.
3 Companies are being forced to **bring out / take out** green products if they want to keep their customers satisfied.
4 We are rapidly **going out of / running out of** fossil fuels.
5 There are very few **poisonous / poisoned** snakes in the wild in this country.
6 **Industrial / Occupational** pollution is reaching dramatic levels in certain parts of the world.

E Use of English: exam practice

Read the text below and decide which answer (A, B, C or D) best fits each gap.

NATURAL DESTRUCTION

For all the talk of what humankind has done to cause destruction to the planet, we should not forget that nature itself is a (1) ___ force, capable of doing damage on a huge scale. The greenhouse (2) ___ and the hole in the ozone layer are indeed made worse by the (3) ___ society we live in. However, we must remember that there are certain (4) ___ of plant and animal which, quite naturally, (5) ___ off gases that are very harmful to the atmosphere. And only 50 years ago in London, hundreds of people died from the (6) ___ which hung over the River Thames. What is interesting here is that, yes, smoke and gases from industry, vehicles and fossil (7) ___ were ingredients in this deadly mixture. The other vital ingredient, though, was the completely natural fog, and who would have thought that could be (8) ___?

In the early days of the industrial revolution, poets, painters and philosophers described how the polluted (9) ___ skies made them think of the end of the world. Well, towards the end of the nineteenth century, the volcanic eruption of Krakatoa nearly made it happen! Thousands of tons of dust and ash were thrown into the air and, for years afterwards, there were red sunsets caused by the light filtering through this natural pollution. Remembering scientists' pet theory about the dinosaurs (10) ___ out because of a huge volcanic eruption, we were lucky that humankind (11) ___ this time.

So, next time you look out from your garden or balcony and see a beautiful red sunset, think of the possibilities. It could be the result of our activities poisoning the air we breathe, or it might just be (12) ___ turning on the radio to check there haven't been any major eruptions lately!

	A	B	C	D
1	**A** heavy	**B** muscular	**C** powerful	**D** natural
2	**A** effect	**B** phenomenon	**C** syndrome	**D** situation
3	**A** commercialised	**B** industrialised	**C** atmospheric	**D** natural
4	**A** races	**B** brands	**C** wildlife	**D** species
5	**A** take	**B** give	**C** throw	**D** run
6	**A** smog	**B** pollutant	**C** sewerage	**D** oxygen
7	**A** flames	**B** fumes	**C** fires	**D** fuels
8	**A** poisoned	**B** harmful	**C** environmental	**D** chemical
9	**A** urban	**B** rural	**C** busy	**D** global
10	**A** killing	**B** dying	**C** fading	**D** going
11	**A** managed	**B** survived	**C** protected	**D** saved
12	**A** while	**B** valuable	**C** worth	**D** good

Reading 2: vocabulary

1 Choose the correct word to complete the sentences.

1 The buzzing of the ______________ kept me awake all night and I got bitten too.
a ladybirds **b** mosquitos **c** grasshoppers **d** beetles

2 You should put some ______________ on your plants to help them grow.
a acid **b** fungus **c** fertiliser **d** trail

3 Bees are insects that live in ______________ .
a colonies **b** trails **c** obstacles **d** eggs

4 Their first job is to ______________ a source of food to ensure survival.
a trail **b** magnify **c** locate **d** found

2 Use a word from the box in each gap to complete the sentences.

critical • intriguing • nomadic • sole • infertile • select • tends • forage

1 They are a ______________ tribe and move from place to place.
2 This plant ______________ to grow better in a sunny spot.
3 You can ______________ which meal you want from the menu.
4 My cat's ______________ interest in life is finding a nice warm place to curl up and sleep.
5 The first few minutes of the turtle's life are ______________ . If it doesn't get to the sea quickly it will be eaten.
6 The foxes often ______________ in our dustbin for scraps of food.
7 If the species becomes ______________ and can't produce young, it will die out.
8 Animal behaviour is a very ______________ field of study.

G Grammar 2

1 If a sentence is correct, put a tick (✔). If it is incorrect, rewrite it correctly.

1 I am looking forward to doing environmental studies at school next year.
2 I wanted to write about zebras for the school project but my teacher wouldn't let me to do it.
3 We stopped to take photographs of the beautiful mountain scenery.
4 This factory stopped to operate years ago because it was causing too much pollution.
5 It is important turning off the tap when you are brushing your teeth because it wastes water.
6 It is my ambition becoming a vet.
7 I would rather going to a natural history museum than a zoo.
8 You would better hurry up or we'll miss the bus to the waterfalls.
9 I would rather they didn't do experiments on animals.
10 I prefer to living in the country rather than in the city.

2 Finish these sentences using ideas of your own about nature and the environment.

1 It is very important for people ______
2 We need to stop ______
3 I would rather ______
4 People should not ______
5 The government should make industries ______
6 Parents should not let their children ______
7 All students should be made ______
8 We can help the environment by ______

E Use of English: exam practice

1 Read the text below and think of the word which best fits each gap. Use only one word in each gap. Write your answers IN CAPITAL LETTERS.

ORNITHOLOGY

Ornithology, or the study of birds, attracts people from all kinds of background. It also attracts a certain amount of ridicule. 'What can be (1) ______ exciting about going out in all weathers looking at birds?' people tend (2) ______ say to me. Well, birds (3) ______ fascinated me since I was young and I would much (4) ______ go out in the rain with my waterproofs and binoculars than sit at home watching television. For those who are still sceptical, (5) ______ sole solution is to get a book on birds, have a quick look, and get out there. Seeing birds in (6) ______ natural environment is so (7) ______ more enjoyable if you know what you are looking at. You don't have to be an expert in order to get pleasure (8) ______ identifying species. Try to avoid making too much noise or the birds will (9) ______ disturbed and fly away and you won't succeed (10) ______ seeing anything.

Oh, and you (11) ______ better take a waterproof jacket – just in case the weather turns bad. Don't worry, though. It'll soon clear (12) ______ and you'll be able to get on with the fascinating hobby of bird-watching.

2 Complete the second sentence so that it has a similar meaning to the first sentence, using the word given. Do not change the word given. You must use between two and five words, including the word given. Write the missing words IN CAPITAL LETTERS.

1 The local environmental organisation has very little money left.
running
The local environmental organisation ______________________________ money.

2 I suggest reading this article before you do your geography homework.
had
You ______________________________ this article before you do your geography homework.

3 Why isn't the government informing people about this problem?
informed
Why ______________________________ about this problem by the government?

4 You'll never manage to convince him that bird-watching is an interesting hobby.
succeed
You'll never ______________________________ him that bird-watching is an interesting hobby.

5 They began this wildlife charity in 1970.
founded
This wildlife charity ______________________________ in 1970.

6 These animals need us if they are going to survive.
depend
These animals ______________________________ their survival.

7 They have said that the company broke several environmental laws.
accused
The company ______________________________ several environmental laws.

8 If we fail to look after the environment, it could end in disaster.
of
If we do not ______________________________ the environment, it could end in disaster.

E Listening: exam practice

CD Track 6 You will hear an interview with a scientist. For questions 1–5, complete the sentences.

Robert Jackson works with (1) ______________ to develop environmental programmes.

Some pollution was caused by (2) ______________ which no longer exist.

Burning (3) ______________ in this area has added to global warming.

They create (4) ______________ after the soil and water have been cleaned.

The area should recover from the problem (5) ______________ .

Revision 1

E Reading: exam practice

You are going to read a magazine article about different ways of learning. For questions 1–15, choose from the sections (A–F). When more than one answer is required, these can be given in any order. The sections may be chosen more than once.

Which section or sections mention(s)

learning by doing?	1 ___	
creative thinkers?	2 ___	3 ___
learning through shapes and images?	4 ___	5 ___
learning best with others?	6 ___	
analytical thinkers?	7 ___	8 ___
needing to move around?	9 ___	
group discussions?	10 ___	11 ___
working with puzzles?	12 ___	13 ___
working best alone?	14 ___	
helping others with problems?	15 ___	

MULTIPLE INTELLIGENCE

Not everyone learns in the same way! Jeffrey Harder describes seven different learning styles, or 'intelligences'. Does one describe your way of learning?

A Verbal or linguistic intelligence, also known as 'word smart', describes a way of learning best through books and words. People with this kind of learning style prefer to learn by reading and writing. They enjoy and are good at both reading and writing stories, poetry, word games and anything else related to words in print. When they take part in discussions with other people, verbal learners tend to think in words instead of pictures and often make notes.

B People with mathematical or logical intelligence favour numbers over words. They are 'maths smart' and like patterns and logic more than words on a page. They excel at puzzles and analysing problems, finding solutions and conducting experiments. They think in numbers and images and look for visual patterns in colour and shapes too. People with this kind of learning style are very systematic and logical thinkers. They are excellent organisers and great at winning arguments!

C People with visual-spatial intelligence learn through images. The expression, 'a picture paints a thousand words' has real meaning to them because they learn best through shapes, pictures and designs that can be seen. Visual learners often like to draw or paint something in order to understand it. They also like puzzles and maps and anything else they can learn from 'seeing'. They are creative learners and often seek careers in fields such as architecture or graphic design.

D Intrapersonal learners are people who can look inside themselves to analyse their thoughts, feelings and beliefs. They enjoy thinking and learning by themselves, and often dislike having to learn in groups with others. Intrapersonal learners are very creative people, strong willed and self-confident. They take time for self-reflection and search for understanding independently. Other people often turn to them for advice and guidance because they can easily analyse and understand personal feelings.

E Interpersonal learners are just the opposite. They prefer to work with other people, face to face. They like the dynamics of being on a team rather than working by themselves. They are 'people smart' and have a great variety of social skills which they use to communicate effectively and interact with others. They are great at taking part in animated discussions. People with interpersonal intelligence have a lot of friends and show genuine understanding for other people. You'll always find them in a group!

F Kinaesthetic learners are 'body smart', which means they learn best by using their body to do something. They don't like to sit still and read about new ideas. They learn best by getting up and doing it themselves. Kinaesthetic learners are very aware of their body's abilities and enjoy physical movement. They learn something by watching someone else do it first, then trying it themselves, like riding a bike or repairing something. Body smart people excel at sports and other activities that keep them moving and doing. They easily become bored when forced to sit still for long periods of time.

E Use of English: exam practice

1 Read the text below and decide which answer (A, B, C or D) best fits each gap.

ALTERNATIVE HOLIDAYS

The concept of exotic holidays is not new. (1) ______________ and other travel packages to tropical locations have long been popular and are more (2) ______________ now than ever. The wealthy have gone on trips to exotic places since the nineteenth century, but now ordinary people have enough money for this kind of holiday. (3) ______________ are increasingly interested in doing something different and want more exciting (4) ______________. A number of tour companies have responded with a new (5) ______________ of options, including African safaris.

Going on safari is a totally (6) ______________ form of holiday. (7) ______________ by a safari guide, groups travel into the African wilderness to experience close up the (8) ______________ of the wild. Being so close to the animals is a once-in-a-lifetime experience. (9) ______________ species, which are (10) ______________ seen outside the zoo, provide a great (11) ______________. On safari, you see the animals in their natural environment, behaving as they do normally. Safaris aren't for everyone, however – especially those who are easily (12) ______________!

	A	B	C	D
1	**A** Decks	**B** Cabins	**C** Traffic	**D** Cruises
2	**A** sensitive	**B** affordable	**C** logical	**D** effective
3	**A** Guides	**B** Spectators	**C** Guests	**D** Holidaymakers
4	**A** journey	**B** trip	**C** travel	**D** movement
5	**A** collection	**B** mixture	**C** range	**D** combination
6	**A** unique	**B** sole	**C** singular	**D** lone
7	**A** Accepted	**B** Delayed	**C** Accompanied	**D** Developed
8	**A** scare	**B** thrill	**C** trauma	**D** fright
9	**A** Environmental	**B** Obsolete	**C** Extinct	**D** Endangered
10	**A** gradually	**B** rarely	**C** only	**D** frequently
11	**A** event	**B** attraction	**C** show	**D** invitation
12	**A** tempted	**B** disgusted	**C** frightened	**D** horrified

2 **Read the text below and think of the word which best fits each gap. Use only one word in each gap. Write your answers IN CAPITAL LETTERS.**

ECO PROJECTS

Schools all (1) ______________ the world are becoming actively involved in environmentally friendly programmes and projects. Many (2) ______________ the projects concern recycling paper and other waste regularly. This helps to conserve and protect our natural resources. The project leaders encourage their students (3) ______________ adopt these habits (4) ______________ home and in their communities, spreading awareness of the need to recycle.

Other schools (5) ______________ gone beyond these traditional measures and are developing more ambitious eco projects. These take many forms and try to raise students' awareness of environmental issues in novel ways. For (6) ______________, recreational areas constructed entirely (7) ______________ of recycled resources are becoming increasingly common. Other projects involve ecological art programmes, (8) ______________ which students make works of art such (9) ______________ sculptures from previously used materials. These are not only beautiful, but also make a statement about how much of what we consume could actually be used again.

All in all, young people today are more aware (10) ______________ ever of the world's dwindling natural resources. They are conscious that they are growing up in a world where environmental problems can no longer be ignored. With the help of their schools, many of them are working together in (11) ______________ to find bright new solutions (12) ______________ old problems.

3 **Read the text below. Use the word given in capitals at the end of some of the lines to form a word that fits in the gap in the same line. Write your answers IN CAPITAL LETTERS.**

One of the things that can be very (1) ______________ when using the internet is	**TIRE**
people's bad (2) ______________ . Because people are often anonymous on the	**BEHAVE**
internet and don't use their real name, they can be very rude and (3) ______________	**KIND**
in a way that they never would be if they were face to face with a person in real life.	
But if you want to know how to deal with these issues and avoid conflict, there are	
some (4) ______________ available on the net. Following 'Netiquette' rules, as	**GUIDE**
they are called, can help make (5) ______________ to how everyone uses the net.	**IMPROVE**
The best way to keep net (6) ______________ friendly is to be polite. Don't use	**RELATION**
Caps Locks. It's the same as shouting. Don't insult people. Don't deliberately try to	
start arguments. People who do this are called trolls and they can be very	
(7) ______________ in the way they get everyone arguing on the net. The only way to	**CREATE**
get rid of a troll is to ignore them. Trolls don't like (8) ______________ as one of their	**ISOLATE**
characteristics is that they want to have the (9) ______________ to annoy everyone.	**FREE**
Don't let them. The best way to make using the net an enjoyable experience is to	
remember that (10) ______________ and politeness go a long way to making any	**HONEST**
community a nice place to be.	

4 Complete the second sentence so that it has a similar meaning to the first sentence, using the word given. Do not change the word given. You must use between two and five words, including the word given. Write the missing words IN CAPITAL LETTERS.

1 Paris is a nice city but it's so expensive.
such
Paris is nice, but it's ______________________ city.

2 Please don't use more water than you really need.
avoid
Please try ______________________ more water than you really need.

3 I'm sure Jane will manage to convince the city council to build a new park.
succeed
I'm sure Jane will ______________________ the city council to build a new park.

4 Sorry, but I couldn't get concert tickets at such short notice.
able
Sorry, but I ______________________ concert tickets at such short notice.

5 'Bringing your own tents on the camping trip isn't necessary,' said Monique.
have
Monique told us we ______________________ our own tents on the camping trip.

6 John advised me to take my studies more seriously.
would
John said, 'If I ______________________ take my studies more seriously.'

7 This trigonometry problem is really hard for me to solve.
work
I can't seem to ______________________ this trigonometry problem.

8 I think Professor Jones started teaching here 100 years ago!
been
I think Professor Jones ______________________ 100 years!

E Listening: exam practice

CD Track 7 You will hear people talking in five different situations. For questions 1–5, choose the best answer (A, B or C).

1 You hear this man talking. What does he regret?
A not doing something sooner
B not earning more money
C not following his original plan

2 You hear this woman talking. Why did she give her hobby up?
A She had no free time.
B She couldn't afford it.
C She found it too difficult.

3 You hear this man talking on the radio. What does he say about modern technology?
A It is a waste of time.
B It stops people communicating.
C It makes people lazy.

4 You hear this teenage girl talking. Who does she blame for the problem?
A her friend
B her mother
C herself

5 You hear this man talking about insects. What does he admire most about them?
A the way they work together
B their ability to survive
C the variety of species

E Writing: exam practice

1 You must answer this question.

You are planning to join a group of students who are touring Italy this summer. Giovanni, the student who will lead the tour, has written to you with information about the places you will visit and how your time will be spent. Below is part of his email. Read the email on which you have made notes. Using the notes you have made, write an email to Giovanni requesting further information.

write reply send

From: giovanni@mailserver.it
Sent: 14th March
Subject: Italy trip

how many students? from where?

On tours like this, all the students really enjoy getting to know each other (which is good because we spend a lot of time together!). We visit a different site every day in a number of different Italian cities.

how much?

During the tour we'll stay in fairly comfortable youth hostels, which include one meal a day in the price. Local restaurants serve famous Italian dishes, so I'm sure you'll find something you like to eat every day!

which meal?

Bring clothes for the Italian summer and don't forget that when we go to places like the Sistine Chapel you must be dressed appropriately.

Please do write back to me if you have any other questions. See you soon!
Ciao!

what does that mean?

Giovanni

Write an email in 120–150 words. You must use grammatically correct sentences with accurate spelling and punctuation in a style appropriate for the situation.

Write an answer to one of the questions 2–4 in this part. Write your answer in 120–180 words in an appropriate style.

2 *Your school magazine is producing a special issue about the local theatre. The editor has asked you to write a review of a play you have seen there recently, mentioning the story, characters and costumes and whether you recommend the play to the magazine's readers.*

Write your review to appear in the magazine.

3 *A magazine for young people is sponsoring a short story competition. The competition rules say that the story must begin with the following words:*

I suddenly realised where I could get the money.

Write your story.

4 *You have recently had a class discussion on the importance of friendship. Now your English teacher has asked you to write an essay, giving your opinions on the following statement:*

Friends are more important to young people than relatives.

Write your essay.

7

Sport

Reading 1: vocabulary

1 Use a word from the box in each gap to complete the sentences.

agility • freestyle • balance • stamina • stunt • teamwork

1 A cross-country runner must have a great deal of _______________ in order to finish the race without becoming exhausted.
2 Gymnasts need an excellent sense of _______________ when jumping and landing on the beam.
3 The key to success is _______________ – everyone working together.
4 Dancers have tremendous _______________ and are able to move their bodies very easily in many ways. Most of us can't do that!
5 _______________ figure skating has always been my favorite winter sport.
6 That was an incredible _______________! How did she do that?

2 Use a word or phrase from the box in the correct form in each gap to complete the text.

devote take off version recreational event skydiving

FOR THE THRILL OF IT!

In the last few years, extreme sports have really (1) _______________. More and more people are out for a thrill and want to try skateboarding and (2) _______________ instead of more traditional (3) _______________ activities. Although plenty of fans are (4) _______________ to their favourite old sports such as football or swimming, (5) _______________ like BMX races draw massive crowds of spectators!
New (6) _______________ of sports seem to be appearing all the time as people push themselves to the limit and go for the biggest thrill!

Grammar 1

1 Choose the correct word or phrase to complete the sentences.

1 Olympic® athletes must **feel / have felt** very proud when they are awarded their medals and hear their national anthem played!
2 Today can't **be / be being** the first time you've played volleyball. You're playing so well.
3 It can't **be / have been** a very good match since half the crowd left the stadium before it even finished.
4 The gymnasts must **be / have been** exhausted after they finished the competition.
5 It couldn't **be / have been** Shareen you saw at the game last night. She's in hospital!
6 You must **like / be liking** bicycle races a lot, since you're always talking about them.

2 Use a form of the words in brackets in each gap to complete the sentences.

1 Tristan ______________ (**ought / bring**) a spare tennis racket with him, so you'll probably be able to play.
2 Tony and Kathy ______________ (**could / play**) golf at the moment, or they might have gone shopping.
3 Dana ______________ (**should / remember**) to call Liz to tell her we postponed the match, so I don't think Liz will turn up.
4 My dad ______________ (**could / go**) to get his bike repaired, but I'm not sure.
5 Last year's team ______________ (**must / be**) a lot better than this year's. They won all their games.
6 The other competitors didn't arrive on time. They ______________ (**might / delay**) by the bad weather.

3 If a sentence is correct, put a tick (✔).

1 The other team should be arriving soon. ☐
2 Dean won first place in the competition again this year! He can't be very happy! ☐
3 If we just practise a little harder, we might stand a chance for the semi-finals. ☐
4 You want to go skydiving? You ought to be mad! ☐
5 My coach told me that I can't have missed another practice or I'm off the team. ☐
6 Your tennis game is really much better. You must have practised a lot since last time we played. ☐

E Use of English: exam practice

Complete the second sentence so that it has a similar meaning to the first sentence, using the word given. Do not change the word given. You must use between two and five words, including the word given. Write the missing words IN CAPITAL LETTERS.

1 I imagine you were extremely happy to be chosen team leader.
must
You ______________________________ extremely happy to be chosen team leader.

2 It's not possible that James signed up for the bungee jumping event!
have
James ______________________________ up for the bungee jumping event!

3 Perhaps Nick has forgotten that practice was cancelled.
might
Nick ______________________________ that practice was cancelled.

4 I don't think Gloria was very happy after she lost the match.
could
Gloria ______________________________ very happy after she lost the match.

5 It's possible that Sarah is running a marathon right now!
may
Sarah ______________________________ a marathon right now!

6 It is possible that Rolf came last, but I really can't remember!
come
Rolf ______________________________ but I really can't remember!

7 I imagine you're getting a little nervous.
be
You ______________________________ a little nervous.

8 You won't have problems finding the gym as it's the only big building in the area.
miss
You ______________________________ the gym as it's the only big building in the area.

E Reading: exam practice

You are going to read a magazine article about whether sport is good for you. Seven sentences have been removed from the article. Choose from the sentences A–H the one which fits each gap (1–7). There is one extra sentence which you do not need to use.

A The sport that causes the most is football.

B Thankfully, this isn't a mainstream sport and only a relatively small number of people do it.

C A lucky few sustain only minor injuries.

D I've looked into injury, deaths and long-term conditions that can be caused by sports.

E The most severe are multiple fractures and head injuries.

F Far more worrying is the effects of doing no exercise at all.

G But there's definitely a case for arguing that sport and exercise can be bad for you too.

H For people who do recreational sports, these types of long-term injuries are far less likely.

Is **sport** good for you?

Stella Jones investigates the dark side of sport and exercise for readers.

The accepted wisdom is that we citizens of the modern world don't get enough exercise. We lead largely sedentary lives where we sit down at work and rarely walk anywhere. That's why health authorities and the sports and lifestyle gurus all insist we need to get up, get out, get moving and do some sport or exercise. But is there any chance that the couch potatoes among us are better off than we imagined? Could it be that it's the healthier lifestyle?

Well, that might be pushing it a bit. [1] Some of you must be a bit sceptical about these claims, so let's have a closer look at them. Then we can decide if the benefits outweigh the damage exercise can do, or not. I've done some research on behalf of our readers to investigate how sport can be bad for you. [2]

The statistics on injury are quite an eye-opener. In Britain, over 13 million people a year receive some kind of injury from doing sport or exercise. [3] But just about any sport or exercise can lead to injury. Most injuries tend to be muscle strains and sprains from over-exertion or poor preparation. While, on the whole, most sports injuries tend to be quite

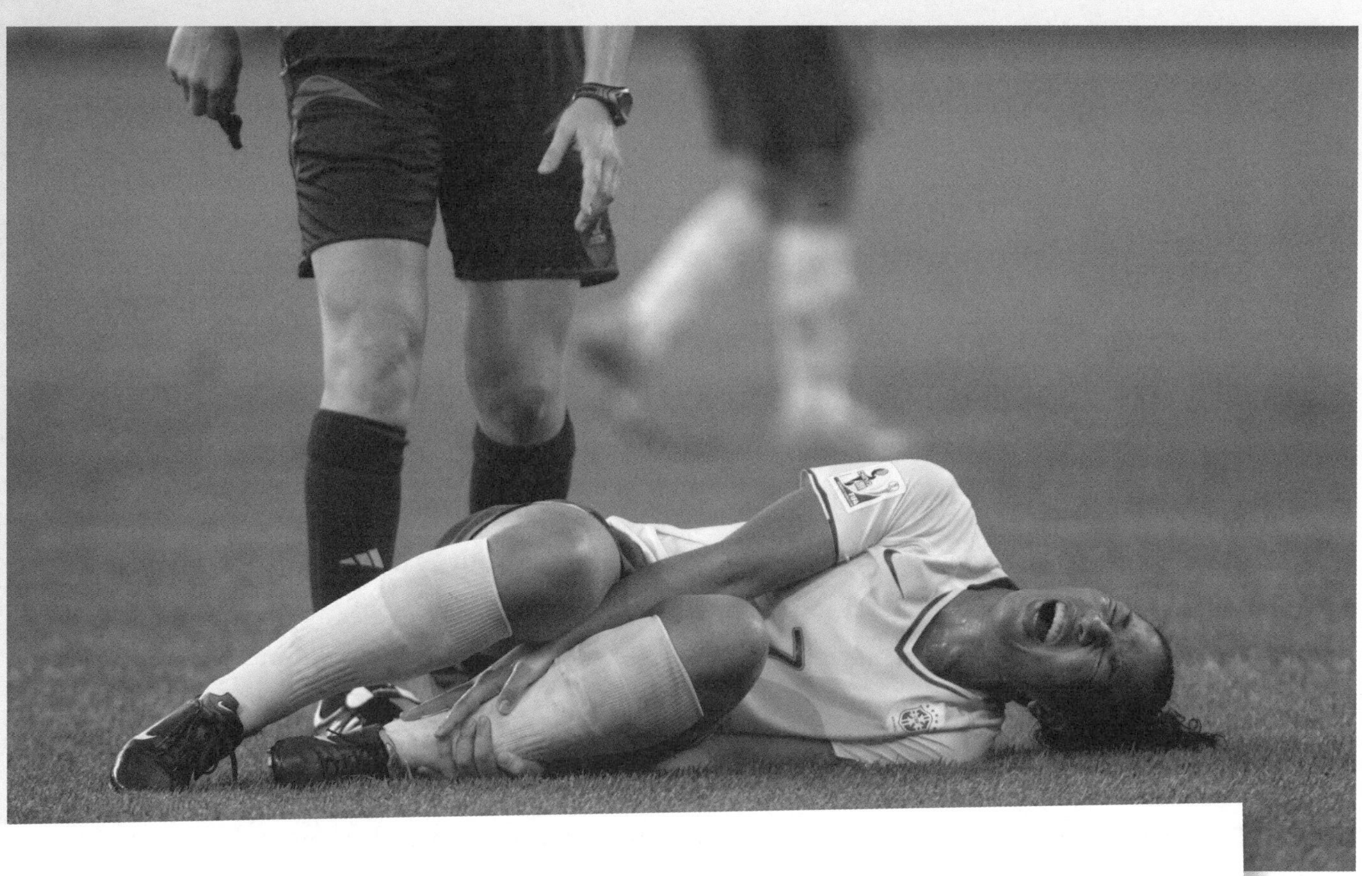

minor, a significant number can be quite serious. 4 These are often caused by such sports as diving, cycling or skiing. Also, over 11 per cent of traumatic spinal injuries, which can lead to paralysis, are the result of a sports injury.

Apart from one-off injuries from sport, there is also the chance that sports enthusiasts will end up with a long-term condition. These are mainly likely to affect professional sports people. Because they play sport at such a high level, they are the ones liable to get a repetitive strain injury (RSI) or do permanent damage to knees or shoulders. 5 Though people who do endurance sports such as long-distance running or cycling as a hobby are also at risk.

Bad as any kind of injury is, the worst case scenario is, of course, death. The most dangerous sport in this respect is base jumping. 6 Of the more popular sports that can be deadly, cycling and swimming are the ones most likely to lead to a fatality. This all makes sport sound pretty scary. But the truth is that the risk of dying from any sport, apart from base jumping, is very low indeed.

Looking at all the data from the comfort of my couch, I have come to the conclusion that doing a sport or exercise can sometimes be a little dangerous. Accidents can happen and people often sprain a wrist or ankle. But the risk of serious injury or death is too small to even think about. 7 This can lead to obesity, heart disease and other serious diseases such as diabetes. Being too much of a coach potato is unhealthy. We all need to do some exercise to be fit and feel good. The key word is moderation.

V Vocabulary

1 Use a word from the box in each gap to complete the text.

coaches • favourites • opponents • referee • team

It was the day of the final! Last year's winning (1) __________ were hungry for another victory, but so were their (2) __________. In fact, having done so well during the season, they were this year's (3) __________ to win. The two sides took to the field with their (4) __________ shouting last-minute directions from the sidelines. The captains shook hands in the middle of the pitch. The (5) __________ blew the whistle and the game was underway!

2 Choose the correct phrasal verbs to complete the sentences.

1 Our girls are down by two points, but there's still time to **drop out / catch up** in the second half.
2 We were a little nervous about **taking on / giving up** last year's champions.
3 As soon as Jerry and I started playing volleyball, the whole gang **caught up / joined in**.
4 Unfortunately, Eva got the flu and had to **put off / drop out** of the competition at the last moment.
5 You must keep one thing in mind while you're training: never **give up / catch up**.
6 Don't **take on / put off** going to the doctor about that ankle. It might be broken.

3 Use a form of the words in brackets in each gap to complete the sentences.

1 Last week's __________ (**lost**) was a great shock to all of us as we'd expected to win.
2 Howard's __________ (**perform**) at yesterday's game was superb and helped us win by five points.
3 Luckily for us, the star player's __________ (**injure**) isn't serious and he'll only miss a couple of games.
4 The Jackson brothers are extremely __________ (**compete**) both on and off the playing field.
5 There's no practice tonight! Save your __________ (**strong**) for tomorrow's game.
6 Hosting the youth basketball games took a lot of __________ (**prepare**) from students and teachers.

4 Use *go, do* or *play* in the correct form in each gap to complete the sentences.

1 Hey, do you want __________ skateboarding this weekend?
2 I used __________ karate when I was younger. I really liked it.
3 Has Mary __________ horse-riding again? She seems to just love it!
4 Why don't we __________ squash after lunch?
5 Last summer, my friends and I __________ windsurfing every chance we got.
6 I think Jeff __________ skiing in the mountains with his family next weekend.
7 You __________ water polo, don't you? I'd love to learn. Can you teach me?
8 It helps to have long legs if you want __________ the high jump.

Reading 2: vocabulary

1 **Match each word 1–5 with its meaning a–e.**

1 rumours	___	**a** supported
2 mood	___	**b** gossip
3 resentment	___	**c** focused
4 reassured	___	**d** atmosphere, feeling
5 single-minded	___	**e** dislike

Use of English: exam practice

Read the text below and decide which answer (A, B, C or D) best fits each gap.

One of the most punishing forms of athletic sport is long-distance running. To be a top marathon runner requires years of (1) ___________ and a lot of (2) ___________. As in most athletic sports, marathon runners are (3) ___________. They do the sport because they are (4) ___________ to it, not to get rich. As it's such a (5) ___________ sport, even people who do it as a hobby need to get into a (6) ___________ of running at least 20 km a day in the run-up to a major race if they are going to have any (7) ___________ of doing well in it. Those marathon runners who want a chance of running in the Olympics® are likely to (8) ___________ someone who can help them gain an edge over their competitors. A good (9) ___________ can make all the difference.

When actually participating in an event, it is vital that long-distance runners (10) ___________ themselves if they want to avoid (11) ___________. But for some runners, all the hard work will (12) ___________ off when they cross the finishing line ahead of the rest of the pack.

1	**A** teaching	**B** learning	**C** training	**D** testing
2	**A** practices	**B** sacrifices	**C** suggestions	**D** resentments
3	**A** athletes	**B** volunteers	**C** champions	**D** amateurs
4	**A** keen	**B** determined	**C** devoted	**D** focused
5	**A** asking	**B** begging	**C** requesting	**D** demanding
6	**A** routine	**B** tradition	**C** custom	**D** design
7	**A** beliefs	**B** prospects	**C** events	**D** actions
8	**A** focus	**B** earn	**C** take on	**D** aim
9	**A** rival	**B** coach	**C** referee	**D** leader
10	**A** pace	**B** speed	**C** race	**D** compete
11	**A** loss	**B** beating	**C** defeat	**D** ruin
12	**A** give	**B** take	**C** run	**D** pay

G Grammar 2

1 Use *at*, *on* or *in* to complete the text.

Far East Studio offers the latest in high intensity martial arts fitness classes. For a serious workout or basic self-defence lessons, we've got what you're looking for. Beginner's classes start (1) ______________ 7am (2) ______________ Mondays and Thursdays (3) ______________ the small gym. Intermediate groups meet (4) ______________ the large gym (5) ______________ the same time (6) ______________ the same days. If you prefer courses (7) ______________ the afternoon and evening, check out our kickboxing programme for all levels beginning (8) ______________ noon and 3pm every day. Advanced courses are held (9) ______________ Wednesdays and Fridays (10) ______________ 9am, 11.30am and 4pm (11) ______________ the large gym. Our spacious facilities are located (12) ______________ our brand new building (13) ______________ the corner of Central St and Greensway Gate (14) ______________ the town centre. Far East Studio is closed only (15) ______________ Christmas and Easter and (16) ______________ the first week of August.

2 Complete each indirect question so that it means the same as the direct question above it.

1 'What time does the game start?'
'Could I ask ______________________________?'
2 'How much are the tickets?'
'Do you know ______________________________?'
3 'Where is seat 43Z?'
'Could you tell me ______________________________?'
4 'How can I meet the team afterwards?'
'I wonder if you might know ______________________________.'
5 'Has my friend Barry arrived yet?'
'Do you think you could ______________________________?'

E Use of English: exam practice

1 Read the text below. Use the word given at the end of some of the lines to form a word that fits in the gap in the same line. Write your answers IN CAPITAL LETTERS.

OLYMPIC® RECORDS

The Olympic Games™ are the most important sports (1) ______________ in the world,	**COMPETE**
with millions of people around the world tuning in to watch them. For spectators, they're	
every four years but the (2) ______________ begin preparing years in advance, in order to	**PARTICIPATE**
give their best (3) ______________ on the day, to try to win a gold medal and perhaps set	**PERFORM**
a world record. The (4) ______________ as to who has actually won must be made with	**DECIDE**
great (5) ______________ , otherwise the wrong person might be declared the winner.	**PRECISE**
In the past, mechanical stopwatches were used by judges for (6) ______________	**TIME**
the athletes, but on many occasions people called their (7) ______________ into	**ACCURATE**
question. In recent years, more modern technology, such as computer timing	
systems and digital (8) ______________ , has been introduced.	**PHOTOGRAPH**
(9) ______________ , this technology allows the judges to give results with much	**FORTUNE**
greater (10) ______________ .	**CERTAIN**

2 Complete each second sentence so that it has a similar meaning to the first sentence, using the word given. Do not change the word given. You must use between two and five words, including the word given. Write the missing words IN CAPITAL LETTERS.

1 Jacob asked a spectator who was winning.
telling
'Would you ______ winning?' Jacob asked a spectator.

2 Susan asked Liz to referee the match.
think
'Do ______ referee the match for us?' said Susan to Liz.

3 What time does the game start?
if
I ______ me what time the game starts.

4 What time did they get to the stadium?
arrived
Could you tell me what time ______ the stadium?

5 Why weren't the girls allowed to play in the match?
prevented
Why were the girls ______ in the match?

6 The International Olympic Committee is also called the IOC.
for
'IOC' ______ 'International Olympic Committee'.

7 Are professional athletes allowed to participate in the Olympics®?
take
Do you know if professional athletes ______ in the Olympics®?

8 This time next week, we'll be at the Cup Final.
time
In ______ we'll be at the Cup Final.

E Listening: exam practice

CD Track 8 You will hear five different people talking about sport at school. For questions 1–5, choose from the list (A–F) what they didn't like about doing sport at school. Use the letters only once. There is one extra letter which you do not need to use.

A You had to do it.	Speaker 1 ___
B It was very competitive.	Speaker 2 ___
C Not many sports were available.	Speaker 3 ___
D The conditions were often unpleasant.	Speaker 4 ___
E It was dangerous.	Speaker 5 ___
F There were no school teams.	

8

Communication

Reading 1: vocabulary

1 Match the adjectives to the nouns to make collocations.

1 Hollywood	___	**a** qualities	
2 text	___	**b** responsibility	
3 visual	___	**c** second	
4 current	___	**d** person	
5 split	___	**e** images	
6 likeable	___	**f** affairs	
7 overall	___	**g** blockbuster	
8 vital	___	**h** messaging	

2 Choose the correct word or phrase to complete the sentences.

1 In many areas of communications, it is important to be able to work to **bulletins / deadlines**.
2 The producer of the war film called in a(n) **explosives / media** expert to deal with the special effects.
3 It is the camera operator's job to **produce / shoot** the scenes, but the editor will decide which ones to use.
4 You have to have a **vital / likeable** personality if you want television viewers to watch you.
5 If you don't **contribute / communicate** any ideas to this report, we'll never get it finished.
6 Newsreaders normally follow a **print / script** but the audience is not always aware of it.

Grammar 1

1 Rewrite the sentences using reported speech.

1 'I am tired of watching television.'
He said ______________________________.
2 'I am trying to listen to the news.'
She said ______________________________.
3 'We sent a text message to Rachel.'
They said ______________________________.
4 'You've used up all the credit on my mobile!'
She said ______________________________.
5 'I have been trying to phone him for hours.'
She said ______________________________.
6 'I was surfing the net yesterday morning.'
He said ______________________________.

2 Write a word or short phrase in each gap to complete the sentences.

1 'I love it here in France.'
He said he loved it ______________ in France.

2 'I can't make it today so it'll have to be tomorrow.'
She said she couldn't make it ______________ so it would have to be ______________ .

3 'I sent you an email yesterday.'
He said he had sent me an email ______________ .

4 'I am starting my media course next month.'
She said she was starting ______________ media course ______________ .

5 'This laptop is mine. My dad gave it to me.'
He said that the laptop was ______________ and that his dad had given it to ______________ .

6 'We can't take it because it's not ours.'
They said that they couldn't take it because it wasn't ______________ .

3 Use the prompts to write sentences in reported speech.

1 Paul / tell / me / last week / he / will be going / on holiday / next day
2 last Saturday / Marsha / say / she / have to work all day / day before
3 David / tell / Matt / last month / he / hope to visit him / following week
4 On Sunday afternoon / Debbie / say / study / all morning
5 when / I / see / Tina / last week / she / say / she / leave for London / that evening
6 John / tell / me / yesterday / you / are / ill

E Use of English: exam practice

Complete the second sentence so that it has a similar meaning to the first sentence, using the word given. Do not change the word given. You must use between two and five words, including the word given. Write the missing words IN CAPITAL LETTERS.

1 'I'm not sure I'll be able to contact you next week.', said Paul. **not**
Paul said he ______________________ be able to contact me the following week.

2 Martin's text message read: 'Sorry. Couldn't find the house.' **had**
Martin sent a text message to say that he ______________________ find the house.

3 'There has been an explosion,' the newsreader said. **that**
The newsreader ______________________ an explosion.

4 'Three years ago I was in the same hotel,' Kevin told me. **before**
Kevin told me that three ______________________ in the same hotel.

5 'Do you know who wrote the original story?' he asked. **had**
He asked me if ______________________ the original story.

6 The message on his answering machine said: 'I am not free right now – please leave your name and number.' **moment**
His answering machine message said he was not ______________________ but I could leave my name and number.

7 'I'll contact you tomorrow,' he said. **following**
He said he ______________________ day.

8 'You must hang up the phone immediately!' she said. **to**
She said ______________________ hang up the phone immediately.

E Reading: exam practice

You are going to read a magazine article about young people and their relationship to new forms of communication and the technology that enables it. For question 1–15, choose from the people (A–D). When more than one answer is required, these can be given in any order. The people may be chosen more than once.

Which person

claims older people don't understand modern methods of communication?	1 ___ 2 ___
points out that social networking isn't as expensive as other methods of communication?	3 ___
has been warned about their online behaviour?	4 ___
believes a gadget they own is a necessity?	5 ___
thinks social networking is easy enough for anyone to use?	6 ___
changed to a different method of communication when the benefits were pointed out?	7 ___
thinks people shouldn't believe everything they read online?	8 ___
acknowledges that aggressive online behaviour is wrong?	9 ___
denies that young people are demanding?	10 ___
uses social networking to maintain contact with family members who live in another country?	11 ___
enjoys teasing people online?	12 ___
doesn't think new methods of communication harm personal relationships?	13 ___
says people communicate differently now?	14 ___ 15 ___

A James

I don't think having a smartphone is a luxury, although my dad would definitely disagree. The last time we discussed it, he told me my generation just thinks it's entitled to get everything it wants. But that's not true. There's no point in denying that it's important for young people to keep up with new technology or risk falling behind in the modern world. I'm not saying that my smartphone isn't a status symbol, as that's part of its appeal. Or that I don't use it for my social life. That would just be silly. The point is that without it, I'd be left out of everything my peers do. Constant communication and social networking are now a part of everyday life for people of my generation. This might be difficult for other generations to grasp but it's true. The way people interact with each other is different nowadays.

B Ally

I first got into social networking in order to keep in touch with relatives abroad. I used to just email them but then my cousin suggested I joined Facebook so that we could all keep in touch at the same time. Now it's all I use, for friends, for family, and I'm in quite a few Facebook groups that are related to the hobbies I do, as well. It's so much better than using email, as far as I'm concerned. I can put pictures on my wall that all my friends can see. I can update my status so that everyone knows what I'm doing and it's completely user-friendly. Even my grandad posts messages on my wall. I think it's a brilliant way of communicating with people and it's a lot cheaper than calling them on the phone.

C Duncan

I use internet forums, chatrooms and social networking as a form of entertainment as much as anything else. It's a great way to meet loads of people and get involved in discussions. Sometimes, I can't resist making fun of some people who use forums because they take everything so seriously and they also fall for anything anyone tells them. It's quite easy to get them annoyed and it's very funny too. I got told off by my parents about doing it, though. They said that I was a troll, which is someone who deliberately starts arguments on the internet for fun. They had a point, but to be honest, I think some people get too involved in forums. It's only the internet. Of course, I realise that sometimes it can get out of hand and that lots of people have been victims of cyber-bullying. I would never get involved in anything like that.

D Moya

I really get annoyed when I hear people say that texting and social networking are destroying personal contact between people. Some people seem to think that only face-to-face contact is real human contact but I disagree strongly. Communication on the net, or by texting, or whatever other form, is still contact. Both ways are great. There are times when I can't see my friends, so I text them, and then we'll meet up at some point. Modern technology has made it possible for me to maintain contact with thousands of people if I want to. No other generation has ever had such an opportunity before. I think people of my parents' age find it difficult to comprehend that you can have lots of different kinds of relationships at the same time. I'm not close friends with all my virtual friends. But so what? It's still great having so many contacts.

V Vocabulary

1 Choose the correct word or phrase.

1 Which of these people would you *not* expect to find working at a TV station?
a presenter **b** newsreader **c** editor **d** viewer

2 Which of these is *not* shown on TV?
a reality TV **b** talk show **c** chat room **d** documentary

3 Which of these is *not* a means of communication?
a email **b** text message **c** studio **d** correspondence

2 Choose the correct word or phrase to complete the sentences.

1 I wish you would **turn / close** that television off.

2 There's a good programme on at nine. Can I **put / turn** over?

3 I have to **bring / hang** up now. Someone's waiting for the phone.

4 As the journalist **turned / took** down notes, the politician looked uncomfortable.

5 You should **bring / turn** up this problem at the next meeting.

6 I'm **getting / putting** you through to Mr Graham, our sales manager.

3 There are twelve words which can be replaced by a form of *get* in the following text. Underline them and write the correct form of *get* above the words.

About a year ago, I decided it was time to buy a new television. My old one (which was almost an antique) had become damaged when we moved house and I could only receive two or three channels clearly. But where was I going to find a new one? I took a bus into town and went straight to the electrical shop. When I arrived there, however, I had a shock. There were so many to choose from that I was lost inside the shop and I didn't know which one to buy. They had become much more complicated over the years. They had also grown bigger, which left me with another problem – how on earth was I going to take it home?

E Use of English: exam practice

Read the text below and decide which answer (A, B, C or D) best fits each gap.

THE RADIO

While the television set is increasingly becoming the focal point of our living rooms, it would be easy to (1) ________ that its older relative, the radio is still there. But in the rush to turn (2) ________ the TV and feast our eyes on all those fantastic visual (3) ________, we are missing out on a valuable (4) ________ of communication.

The radio has all the talk (5) ________, comedies, dramas and news (6) ________ that the television has, and more besides. Late night shows have (7) ________ presenters to keep you awake or send you to sleep, depending on your needs.

Hard-hitting reporters (8) ________ the hot items of the day with politicians and experts in specialised areas. And behind the (9) ________ there are researchers and editors making sure you get the (10) ________ up-to-date information.

With the new generation of digital radio entering our homes via satellite, radio is sure to (11) ________ to our lives well into the future. The radio of tomorrow will guarantee perfect (12) ________ and more choice of programme.

	A	B	C	D
1	**A** insist	**B** notice	**C** suggest	**D** forget
2	**A** on	**B** up	**C** off	**D** down
3	**A** pictures	**B** images	**C** appearances	**D** looks
4	**A** way	**B** direction	**C** means	**D** approach
5	**A** events	**B** discussions	**C** performances	**D** shows
6	**A** bulletins	**B** episodes	**C** documentaries	**D** breaks
7	**A** personal	**B** likeable	**C** likely	**D** presentable
8	**A** converse	**B** correspond	**C** discuss	**D** enthuse
9	**A** scenes	**B** shots	**C** films	**D** camera
10	**A** soonest	**B** latest	**C** greatest	**D** biggest
11	**A** give	**B** contribute	**C** donate	**D** lend
12	**A** reception	**B** receipt	**C** recipe	**D** recital

Reading 2: vocabulary

1 Use a word from the box in each gap to complete the sentences.

proportion • pioneer • merge • exceed • slump • deleted • instant • emails

1 Don't ever open ______________ if you don't know who they're from.
2 The ______________ of people who don't have a mobile is very small nowadays.
3 Steve Jobs was a ______________ of the digital age.
4 Smartphones are useful because they ______________ several gadgets together in one.
5 I accidentally ______________ your number so can you give it to me again, please?
6 If you ______________ the free call time, it can be quite expensive.
7 There's been no ______________ in the sale of digital gadgets this year.
8 I use Facebook for ______________ messaging all the time.

2 For each word or phrase, write a word or phrase with a similar meaning. Some letters have been given to help you.

1 talking to workmates on electronic equipment v______________ c______________
2 people who pay to access a service s______________
3 online forums used to keep in touch with people s______________ n______________ s______________
4 old-fashioned o______________
5 removed slowly p______________ o______________
6 discounts or bargains u______________ o______________
7 suitable a______________

G Grammar 2

1 Match the phrases to make sentences.

1 Anne is going to register for the computer course despite ___
2 He kept chatting online even though ___
3 John does not have virus protection on his computer although ___
4 She continues to spend hours on the internet in spite ___

a of the fact that her parents don't like it.
b the fact that it is very expensive.
c he had school the next morning.
d he knows it is very risky.

2 If a sentence is correct, put a tick (✔). If it is incorrect, rewrite it correctly.

1 He claimed that to be an expert on computers but he nearly destroyed mine.
2 Despite of the cost, I really want to get a laptop.
3 He managed to install the program in spite of the difficulty.
4 The thief denied to steal my mobile.
5 I refuse to write another email until he answers my last one.
6 They told to me that the computer would cost a fortune to fix.
7 Ben suggested going to the internet café.
8 We agreed paying half each for the phone bill.

3 Use a word from the box in each gap to complete the phrases.

deny • ask • claim • agree • suggest • refuse • tell

1 __________ / __________ to do something
2 __________ / __________ doing something
3 __________ / __________ someone to do something
4 __________ that something is true

E Use of English: exam practice

1 Read the text below. Use the word given in capitals at the end of some of the lines to form a word that fits in the gap in the same line. Write your answers IN CAPITAL LETTERS.

WRITING FOR THE SCREEN

You don't really need any formal (1) __________ to write a film, television or radio script **QUALIFY**
as it's the quality of the script that counts, not what you have studied. However, you do need
good (2) __________ skills and it will also certainly be useful if you have a vivid **COMMUNICATE**
(3) __________ . This will help you to come up with a plot. Once you have done that, **IMAGINE**
your job is to make what happens as real and (4) __________ as possible. To do that, you **BELIEVE**
will need to watch people very (5) __________ to see how they act. Ask yourself how **CLOSE**
they demonstrate their emotions when they are sad, angry, surprised or (6) __________ . **ENTHUSE**
Notice where they put their hands when they are deep in (7) __________ . Pay attention **DISCUSS**
to how different people express themselves in an (8) __________ . Focus on the different **ARGUE**
ways people start and finish a (9) __________ . These are the kinds of areas you need to **CONVERSE**
be looking at because the difference between fascinated viewers and bored viewers rests on
(10) __________ like these. **OBSERVE**

2 Complete the second sentence so that it has a similar meaning to the first sentence, using the word given. Do not change the word given. You must use between two and five words, including the word given. Write the missing words IN CAPITAL LETTERS.

1 My phone doesn't have a camera on it, even though it's quite new.
fact
In ______________________ my phone's quite new, it doesn't have a camera on it.

2 Tony said that he wouldn't send the email for me.
refused
Tony ______________________ the email for me.

3 'Why don't you give Madison a call?' Alice said.
suggested
Alice ______________________ Madison a call.

4 Despite the fact that I don't make many calls, my phone bill is always quite high.
making
In spite ______________________ many calls, my phone bill is always quite high.

5 Did you believe Jenny's claim that she is a spy?
to
Did you believe Jenny when ______________________ a spy?

6 Are you trying to say that you didn't steal her mobile phone?
deny
Are you trying ______________________ her phone?

7 'Sit down, John!' his teacher said.
to
John's teacher ______________________ sit down.

8 Despite having to spend so much time on the phone, I like my new job.
even
I like my new job, ______________________ spend so much time on the phone.

E Listening: exam practice

CD Track 9 You will hear part of an interview about a new newspaper. For questions 1–5, choose the best answer (A, B or C).

1 Susan says *The Daily Post* is similar to a tabloid newspaper because it
A has lots of stories about celebrities.
B has millions of readers.
C is quite small.

2 Susan says *The Daily Post* is different to many newspapers because it is
A only for younger readers.
B also for younger readers.
C not for younger readers.

3 What does Susan say about *The Daily Post* and politics?
A The paper isn't interested in politics.
B The paper supports a political party.
C The paper doesn't support a political party.

4 What does Susan say about *The Tuesday Magazine?*
A It should have fewer advertisements.
B It should have more pages.
C It should be cheaper.

5 What might happen soon, according to Susan?
A *The Daily Post* will drop its price.
B *The Daily Post* will sell fewer copies.
C *The Daily Post* will face strong competition.

9

Work

Reading 1: vocabulary

1 Match each word or phrase 1–7 with a meaning a–g.

1 typical	___	**a** possible
2 cash flow	___	**b** experienced
3 mature	___	**c** collecting
4 potential	___	**d** finances
5 handle	___	**e** deal with
6 undertaking	___	**f** starting to do
7 gathering	___	**g** average

2 Use a word from the box in the correct form in each gap to complete the sentences.

franchise • earn • position • hire • errand • like-minded • income • straightforward

1 Carlo ______________ a lot of money last summer as a golf caddy.
2 I got tired of being a waiter so the restaurant offered me a new ______________ : dishwasher!
3 My mum asked me to run a few ______________ for her on my way to work today.
4 Nick and I are very ______________ and both want to start a garden-care business together.
5 Mary thought the job of manager's assistant would be pretty ______________ but it turned out to be really complicated.
6 I don't think they'll ______________ me at the newsagent's unless I cut my hair shorter.
7 I took a part-time job because I wanted a little ______________ of my own.
8 Have you ever worked for a big ______________ ? I hear the benefits are really great!

Grammar 1

1 If a sentence is correct, put a tick (✔).

1 Margaret Davis who lives next door to my mother works with my brother at the supermarket. ☐
2 Mr Thomas is the manager of Buba's Burgers which opened last month in the town centre. ☐
3 I'd like to be hired as waitress, which is fairly well-paid work. ☐
4 The woman who hired Steve told him he had a bright future with Donut Queen. ☐
5 Ms Andu, who called you about the job, is a very nice person. ☐
6 The position, that is advertised in the paper, requires more experience than I have. ☐

2 Choose the correct word or phrase to complete the sentences.

1 That modern building over there is the one ______________ my mum works.
a which **b** where **c** that

2 Monica, ______________ is my new boss, is very easy to work with.
a whose **b** that **c** who

3 The biggest reason ______________ I didn't take the job is the low pay.
a which **b** why **c** when

4 This is the employees' lounge, ______________ you can keep your things while you're working.
a where **b** which **c** that

5 I'd rather take the assistant manager's position, ______________ offers much better pay.
a that **b** which **c** who

6 My co-worker, ______________ name is Salvatore, comes from Italy.
a that **b** who's **c** whose

3 Write a–f in each gap to complete the sentences.

1 Kristina, ____ , was offered her job back today!
2 I work for a really small internet company, ____ .
3 Tom works for a computer company ____ .
4 Mindy, ____ , wants to be one too when she's older.
5 Isaac met Alex at a job fair ____ .
6 Did Jack give you any reason ____ ?

a where they both went to learn about career opportunities
b that hires teenagers for part-time positions
c which makes me feel like I'm part of a family
d why he left his job so suddenly
e who quit her job last weekend
f whose mother is a lawyer

4 Combine the two sentences to form one sentence containing a relative clause.

Example:
Carlos is very hard-working. (He works for a large multinational company.)
Carlos, who works for a large multinational company, is very hard-working.

1 Jean and Toby are coming to dinner tonight. (They are colleagues of mine.)

____

2 That office is the biggest in the building. (It is Mr Phillipson's.)

____

3 Dave wasn't offered the job. (It's a shame.)

____

4 My new assistant seems very efficient. (His name is Gareth.)

____

5 The old factory is for sale. (Bob used to work there.)

____

6 Tracy didn't come to work today. (Elaine told me she's leaving the company.)

____

E Reading: exam practice

You are going to read an article about teens at work. Seven sentences have been removed from the article. Choose from the sentences A–H the one which fits each gap (1–7). There is one extra sentence which you do not need to use.

A Other people have seen me on the street and that's how I got more work.

B When I show them to people I can see that they feel like they've made a discovery or something, and that's kind of exciting.

C It was the best solution for me at this time.

D I understand them and they trust me.

E It gives me something really enjoyable to do with my free time and I get to meet lots of people.

F Well, when it rains I guess it's a little boring, because there aren't many people around.

G Luckily, my studies prepared me for this perfectly.

H That's where I come in.

ON THE JOB!

Have you ever thought about taking on part-time work for a little pocket money and some good experience? Allison Seeley takes a peek at eight working teenagers to find out who's doing what on the job!

Patty is 16 and started working as a volunteer in her local hospital last year. Although she's not paid, she says there are a lot of benefits to her work. She had thought about studying to be a doctor when she was younger, and now is really sure about it. 'I see the doctors in action every day, and I dream about living a life like theirs,' says Patty.

Mara has been in the school swimming team for years, so when a part-time job opened up at the pool, she was interested. Now she works part-time teaching children how to swim. 'Since I'm in the pool all the time anyway, I might as well get paid a bit too,' she laughs. 'I can remember being afraid of the water when I was little, so I really enjoy helping kids become good swimmers. 1 ____ That's what makes it all worthwhile, really.'

On Saturday and Sunday afternoon, you'll find Mike in the park. Don't look for him on the playing field, however; Mike's in a kiosk, working. Mike's parents have run the kiosk in the park for many years now, so it was only natural for Mike to join them. 'While I'm still a student,' he explains, 'it's a perfect part-time job. My friends stop by and chat, I can watch all the games and I get to enjoy the sunny weather. 2 ____ Then I get a little time to read or play video games or something. I don't really mind.'

'I have the funniest job in the world,' says Josie, as an enormous Saint Bernard pulls her along the street. 'I'm a dog walker! It happened quite by accident really. A neighbour asked me to walk her dog when she was suffering from a cold, then it just became a habit! 3 ___ I love animals so it's lots of fun. I can hardly believe I get paid for walking other people's dogs, but it really does help them out.'

Sarah used to babysit often, but then she specialised in caring for young babies. 'Most mums won't leave their newborn baby with a babysitter, but they still need help with them. 4 ___ I've learned all about caring for infants through books, classes and on-the-job training, so I feel very comfortable and confident with them,' she says. She helps take care of three infants right now, visiting their houses for an hour or so whenever the mums need her assistance.

Roy got a job at a nearby car wash to help earn money for college next year. He works at the weekend, drying the cars as they emerge from the car wash. 'It may not be the most exciting job in the world,' he admits, 'but the money is good and the hours are right. 5 ___ I've saved quite a bit of money already and I'm looking forward to going away to university next year.'

Scott's a bit of a bookworm, so a part-time job at the public library was ideal for him. 'I love books of all kinds, especially the older editions and rare books. 6 ___' Scott works almost every day after school for a few hours, so it doesn't interfere with his schoolwork or time with his friends. 'It's perfect really,' he says, 'and I get a lot of time to read the books that I like.'

'I love having a job,' beams Molly from behind the ice-cream counter, struggling with a scoop of frozen strawberry ice cream. ' 7 ___' Molly likes her job because it's a happy environment where people come for fun. 'People go out for ice cream when they're feeling good about something or just need a break, so most of my customers are friendly and smiling. I like that.'

V Vocabulary

1 Match each word or phrase in 1–12 with a meaning in a–l.

1 being unemployed ___
2 being self-employed ___
3 permanent ___
4 temporary ___
5 being on commission ___
6 royalties ___
7 salary ___
8 wage ___
9 commuting ___
10 going on a business trip ___
11 doing overtime ___
12 being on strike ___

a forever, for a long time
b travelling to and from work every day
c refusing to work in order to bring about change
d working more hours than the standard working day or week
e the amount of money you make in a year, usually paid every month
f getting paid for every sale you make
g not having a job
h travelling for a few days to do work in another place, then returning
i providing a service or running your own company
j the amount of money you earn per hour or week
k the money an author or songwriter, etc, earns
l short term

2 Use a phrasal verb from the box in the correct form in each gap to complete the sentences.

fill in • take on • take up • take over • put in

1 I ______________ for a raise last month and I actually got it! Let's go out and celebrate!
2 Make sure you ______________ the application form correctly, or it will make a bad impression.
3 When Maggie became manager, she ______________ a lot more responsibility.
4 I've heard that a much larger company might ______________ our firm.
5 Answering the phones at work ______________ a lot of my time. Sometimes it's all I can do!

3 Use a form of the words in brackets in each gap to complete the sentences.

1 Frankly, you are by far the best ______________ (**apply**) for the job; I'd like to make you an offer.
2 Ms Snyder is busy right now, but you can speak to her personal ______________ (**assist**) if you like.
3 The ______________ (**manage**) director of our company has a great deal of responsibility.
4 When you first start your job, there will be a three-week ______________ (**train**) period so you can learn exactly what you need to do.
5 Last month, Thomas was promoted to ______________ (**supervise**). Now he's our boss!
6 Business is going so well that we hired seven new ______________ (**employ**) in our department last month.
7 John's father was a railway ______________ (**work**) for many years. He helped lay the tracks for the new inter-city train system.

4 Use *have, take, make* or *do* in the correct form in each gap to complete the sentences.

1 I ______________ an appointment with the careers adviser at school yesterday.
2 My brother got a job ______________ research for a pharmaceutical company.
3 If I ______________ the chance to be anything in the world, I'd be an astronaut.
4 My mum says that ______________ the housework is like having a full-time job!
5 I'll wait until I'm at university before ______________ a decision about what career to follow.
6 Jeff didn't really like his summer job, but he ______________ the best of it and had some fun.
7 Last week you wanted to be a teacher, now you want to be a doctor! Would you ______________ up your mind!
8 You've been working so hard lately, why don't you ______________ a break?
9 When you're lifting heavy boxes in the office, ______________ care not to hurt your back.

Reading 2: vocabulary

1 Match each word or phrase 1–6 with a meaning a–f.

1 earn	___	**a**	end result
2 share	___	**b**	something taken for granted
3 co-exist	___	**c**	receive money for work
4 outcome	___	**d**	give or provide
5 contribute	___	**e**	divide / split
6 a given	___	**f**	happen or be at the same time

2 Read the text below and decide which answer (A, B, C or D) best fits each gap.

STARTING WORK

In recent years, job markets have become so competitive that choosing the right (1) ________ path has become crucial for many young people. The goal of most young people is to find a (2) ________ that offers some decent benefits. The most basic of these is a good (3) ________ but also includes such things as paid holiday leave, health insurance and a (4) ________ fund. But often the reality is somewhat different. Many young people are having to work for a low (5) ________ of pay, with no extra payment for (6) ________ and with the threat that they could be (7) ________ redundant at any time. It's no wonder that there is low morale among many (8) ________ these days.

This has lead a growing number of young people to show (9) ________ and start up their own businesses offering a whole range of (10) ________ to people who live in their (11) ________ communities. It requires a lot of (12) ________ and some luck but it can pay off in the end.

	A	B	C	D
1	**A** job	**B** career	**C** vocation	**D** occupation
2	**A** station	**B** spot	**C** position	**D** location
3	**A** salary	**B** earnings	**C** return	**D** compensation
4	**A** wealth	**B** benefit	**C** fortune	**D** pension
5	**A** figure	**B** charge	**C** rate	**D** cost
6	**A** functions	**B** work	**C** occasions	**D** overtime
7	**A** taken	**B** forced	**C** made	**D** done
8	**A** assistants	**B** employees	**C** bosses	**D** labours
9	**A** operation	**B** adventure	**C** concern	**D** enterprise
10	**A** services	**B** proposals	**C** suggestions	**D** projects
11	**A** close	**B** nearby	**C** local	**D** residential
12	**A** exercise	**B** strain	**C** force	**D** effort

G Grammar 2

1 Use a word or phrase from the box in the correct form in each gap to complete the text.

cut • do • make up
dye • massage • lift

ZINA'S NEW AGE BODY SPA

Come to Zina's and have your spirits (1) ______________ by the soothing services we provide. For total relaxation, have your body (2) ______________ by Jorgen, our expert Swedish masseur. Then have your hair (3) ______________ and (4) ______________ for an exciting new look! Don't stop there! Zina's is a full service salon where you can have a manicure (5) ______________ and your face (6) ______________ in time for lunch with your friends!

2 Use a word from each box in the correct form to tell a new neighbour what services are available in your neighbourhood.

films • dresses • eyes • shirts • car • hair

cut • develop • make • check • clean • repair

In our neighbourhood, you can have your …

1 ______________ at the optician's on Maple Street.
2 ______________ by the tailor next to the bank.
3 ______________ at the photo shop by the fast-food restaurant.
4 ______________ at the hairdressing salon on Main Street.
5 ______________ at the cleaners next to the post office.
6 ______________ at the garage on the corner of Pine Street.

3 Use the causative to complete the second sentence so that it has the same meaning as the first.

1 Mr Fergus, the farmer, removed a cherry tree from our garden.
We ______________
2 They paid three stone workers to rebuild their garden wall.
They ______________
3 Mark and Julie went to a professional photographer for their wedding pictures.
Mark and Julie ______________
4 I asked them to renew my subscription to *Nirvana* magazine last week.
I ______________
5 It is very expensive to repair a Rolls-Royce.
Having ______________
6 A thief stole my sister's camera yesterday.
My sister ______________

4 Use the words in brackets in the correct form in each gap to complete the sentences. Add any other necessary words.

1 Margot wants to ______________ (**portrait / paint**) by a well-known local artist.
2 I was thinking about ______________ (**hair / dye**) a different colour. What do you think?
3 We ______________ (**TV / repair**) last week and it's still not working properly.
4 Gloria ______________ (**braces / remove**) tomorrow. I hope her teeth look fantastic!
5 Audrey ______________ (**hours / reduce**) at work recently so she can study more.
6 Did you ______________ (**hat / design**) for you?

E Use of English: exam practice

1 Read the text below and think of the word which best fits each gap. Use only one word in each gap. Write your answers IN CAPITAL LETTERS.

THE SUMMER JOB

Last summer, when I was looking (1) ______________ a part-time job, I found two interesting adverts in the paper. The first job was at the library, (2) ______________ I thought sounded a little boring. The second ad was for a nearby animal hospital. How hard could that be? I like animals, so I (3) ______________ up my mind to apply (4) ______________ the position of 'animal caretaker', not really knowing what the job involved. I (5) ______________ an appointment for an interview right away. When I arrived, I filled (6) ______________ the application form with the secretary, then waited to be called in by the office manager, Mrs Kaneen, (7) ______________ was doing the interviews. When she asked me if I (8) ______________ any experience with animals, I said yes. She smiled, told me (9) ______________ much the pay was, which sounded great, so I decided to (10) ______________ the job. Mrs Kaneen told me to start right away (11) ______________ cleaning out the dog kennels. When I finished, I was to act as the vet's assistant during some operations. That's when I realised that I had taken (12) ______________ far more than I could manage!

2 Complete the second sentence so that it has a similar meaning to the first sentence, using the word given. Do not change the word given. You must use between two and five words, including the word given. Write the missing words IN CAPITAL LETTERS.

1 I want you to try as hard as you can to finish the project on time. **best**
I want you to ______________________________ to finish the project on time.

2 That man's sister made a fortune on the stock exchange. **is**
That ______________________________ made a fortune on the stock exchange.

3 My job doesn't leave me enough free time. **takes**
My job ______________________________ of my time.

4 Did you hear that Ted was fired last week? **sack**
Did you hear that Ted ______________________________ last week?

5 If that tooth is really bothering you, maybe a dentist should take it out. **have**
You should ______________________________ if it's really bothering you.

6 My family's company is being purchased by a large international firm. **over**
A large international firm ______________________________ my family's company.

7 I didn't have anything to do with the strike last month. **take**
I didn't ______________________________ last month's strike.

8 Did many people apply for the job? **lot**
Were ______________________________ for the job?

E Listening: exam practice

CD Track 10 You will hear an interview with a writer. For questions 1–5, complete the sentences.

Craig Danton wrote his first novel at (1) ______________ .

Craig says his first novel didn't have a good plot or well-developed (2) ______________ .

Craig got seventeen (3) ______________ from publishers.

Craig says an unpublished writer has to have (4) ______________ in order to find a publisher.

Craig's success in a (5) ______________ led to him getting his second novel published.

10

Health

Reading 1: vocabulary

1 Use a word from the boxes in each gap to complete the sentences.

agony • hysterical • panic • emergencies

1 The one thing you should never do in ________ is to ________. The last thing someone in ________ needs is to be assisted by someone who is ________.

inadequate • assessment • clutching • hesitate

2 She was lying on the ground ________ her ankle. Even though my knowledge of first aid was ________, I didn't ________ to make an ________.

bleeding • cope with • ran out • unconscious

3 I ________ into the street and found the boy lying ________ in the road. He was also ________ from his nose. I really didn't know how to ________ the situation.

broken bones • suppress • goes beyond • cuts and bruises

4 The training course ________ what you learn in basic medical training such as how to deal with minor ________. You have to learn to ________ your fears and be prepared to treat ________ and other more serious injuries.

2 Match each word or phrase 1–5 with a meaning a–e.

1 fractures	___	**a**	the worst news
2 beaming	___	**b**	memory loss
3 sobering	___	**c**	shining brightly
4 killer blow	___	**d**	broken bones
5 amnesia	___	**e**	serious – makes you think

Grammar 1

1 Tick (✓) the boxes next to the correct statements.

1 If I had known about the new restaurant, I wouldn't have ordered the takeaway.
- ☐ I knew about the restaurant.
- ☐ I didn't know about the restaurant.
- ☐ I ordered a takeaway.
- ☐ I didn't order a takeaway.

2 If you were right, he would be answering the phone.
- ☐ You were wrong.
- ☐ You are wrong.
- ☐ He isn't answering the phone.
- ☐ He will answer the phone.

3 Had you told me in advance, I would have been happy to come.
- [ ] You didn't tell me.
- [ ] You told me.
- [ ] I wasn't happy to come.
- [ ] I didn't come.

4 Had it not been for Damian, we wouldn't be here now.
- [ ] Damian does something.
- [ ] Damian did something.
- [ ] We aren't here now.
- [ ] We are here now.

2 Match to make sentences.

1 Had you decided sooner,
2 If it hadn't been for Eileen's first aid skills,
3 If you were eighteen,
4 Were I his doctor,
5 If he were really ill,
6 If you hadn't been so greedy at the restaurant,

a you'd be in hospital now.
b I would have advised him to stay in bed.
c you wouldn't be feeling sick now.
d you could have joined the gym for half price.
e he wouldn't have gone to the cinema last night.
f you would have been allowed to give blood yesterday.

3 Use a word from the box in each gap to complete the text. Use some of the words more than once.

if • had • have • been • would • were • be • getting

(1) __________ we known, back in the old days, a little bit more about metals, we could (2) __________ avoided quite a few health problems. Firstly, if we (3) __________ known that lead, the metal used for most of our water pipes, was poisonous, surely we would have (4) __________ able to find an alternative, rather than slowly poisoning generations of people. (5) __________ we had known more about iron, on the other hand, we (6) __________ have realised that it is a metal which was actually helping our health. Many cooking utensils and pans used to be made of iron and, just by using them in food preparation, we were adding tiny amounts of iron to our diet. (7) __________ we to still use iron pots and pans today, it would (8) __________ beneficial. (9) __________ we hadn't discovered aluminium and stainless steel, most of us would still be (10) __________ our daily requirement of iron, without the need to take it in tablet form.

E Use of English: exam practice

Complete the second sentence so that it has a similar meaning to the first sentence, using the word given. Do not change the word given. You must use between two and five words, including the word given. Write the missing words IN CAPITAL LETTERS.

1 It was thanks to my doctor that I made such a quick recovery. **would**
If it hadn't been ______________________________ not have recovered so quickly.

2 Thank goodness you knew first aid; he nearly died! **known**
If you ______________________________ he might have died.

3 You were ill because you ate so much! **have**
You would ______________________________ you hadn't eaten so much!

4 I didn't realise how important it was; otherwise I would have taken the tablets. **realised**
I would have taken the tablets, ______________________________ so important.

5 You should speak to him – he'll listen to you. **to**
Were ______________________________ he would listen.

6 I can't play football with you because I have this awful cold. **able**
If I didn't have this awful cold, ______________________________ to play football with you.

7 It's possible that you would have avoided the illness if you had stayed at home. **might**
You ______________________________ ill if you had stayed at home.

8 I had to go to the doctor because my symptoms were very worrying. **had**
I ______________________________ to go to the doctor if my symptoms hadn't been so worrying.

E Reading: exam practice

You are going to read a magazine article about dieting. For questions 1–8, choose the answer (A, B, C or D) which you think fits best according to the text.

1 How do the weight-gain diets of sports players and patients differ?
- **A** Sports players, unlike patients, focus on their own personal weight levels.
- **B** Sports players, unlike patients, are interested in increasing their strength.
- **C** Patients try to increase muscle and body fat, rather than just muscle.
- **D** Patients try to get back weight they have lost rather than put on extra weight.

2 The phrase 'In effect' (line 22) suggests that
- **A** De Niro's diet was particularly effective and successful.
- **B** although De Niro may not have described it as a diet, it was.
- **C** De Niro made a very great effort to reduce the weight he had gained.
- **D** changing your eating patterns does not always lead to effective weight loss.

3 According to the writer, a lot of people wrongly believe that
- **A** you shouldn't aim to reduce your body fat in a weight-loss diet.
- **B** the only effect of eating less is a decrease in the amount of body fat.
- **C** successful weight loss comes through losing muscle, water and fat.
- **D** if you eat less, your body may actually lose muscle rather than fat.

4 Some dieters do pushups, according to the writer, to ensure that
- **A** they have enough protein in their bodies.
- **B** their muscles aren't restricted in any way.
- **C** they don't lose muscle instead of fat.
- **D** they are able to lift heavy weights.

5 The 'most sensible weight-loss diet' (lines 42–43) involves
- **A** eating smaller amounts of normal food, and choosing healthier alternatives.
- **B** adapting portions so that the diet is more balanced than normal.
- **C** replacing all fatty foods with their non-fat alternatives.
- **D** increasing the size of some portions, and decreasing others.

6 What does the writer mean by 'obtain satiation' (line 57)?
- **A** stop you eating unhealthy and fatty food
- **B** stop you losing your appetite for vegetables
- **C** make you feel like you have eaten enough
- **D** make you only want to eat healthy vegetables

7 How does Weight Watchers differ from Overeaters Anonymous?
- **A** Weight Watchers is more worried about advertising.
- **B** Weight Watchers is a business that tries to make a profit.
- **C** Overeaters Anonymous is less successful at making money.
- **D** Overeaters Anonymous isn't interested in helping individuals.

8 According to the writer, what is the Atkins Diet a good example of?
- **A** a diet that was in fashion but isn't anymore
- **B** a diet that was promoted by celebrities
- **C** a diet that all scientists agree is very good
- **D** a diet that some doctors do not recommend

GOING ON A DIET?

Dora Stephenson asks what people really mean when they say they're 'going on a diet'.

If someone tells you they're going on a diet, the chances are you'll imagine they're trying to lose weight. In fact, weight-loss diets are only one type of dieting. Some sports players, for example, might go on a weight-gain diet, with the aim of increasing their body mass and, by extension, their strength. Patients who have lost weight through illness may also embark on a weight-gain diet. Their aim differs from the athlete in that they're attempting to return to their previous levels of muscle and body fat, rather than aiming to increase their normal personal levels. Actors may also decide to go on a weight-gain diet to play a particular role. Robert De Niro, for example, is well known for greatly increasing his weight to play certain characters – he gained more than 27 kilograms to play the older La Motta in the film *Raging Bull*.

At the end of filming, De Niro presumably changed his eating patterns to reduce his
22 weight. In effect, he went on a weight-loss
diet. Weight-loss diets generally limit the amount of certain foods, or food in general, in order to reduce body mass. Despite what many people think, this reduction is not just a reduction in fat, however. Weight loss is usually a combination of a loss in muscle, water and fat. Indeed, some dieters lose weight without losing much fat at all. An overweight person dieting should aim to lose fat rather than muscle. Some dieters therefore have to restrict their muscle loss by doing pushups, lifting weights and making sure they get enough protein (which is required to build muscle).

Protein is just one of the essential nutrients our bodies need. We also need fats, vitamins, minerals and water. A diet that doesn't provide these nutritional requirements can be damaging to our physical well-being. In
42 general, then, the most sensible weight-loss
diet is an adapted standard balanced diet – adapted in the sense that the size of portions is reduced, and some foods are substituted for others (for example, full-fat milk is replaced with skimmed milk, or sugar is replaced with artificial sweetener).

Although some overweight people are overweight because of their metabolism, others are overweight simply because they eat too much. For this reason, some diets focus on the psychological aspect of weight loss, with the aim of reducing the desire to overeat. Some foods, for example high-fibre vegetables, have been shown to
effectively 'obtain satiation', or, in other 57
words, to create a feeling of fullness and loss of appetite. Drinking water and exercising are also effective in reducing the appetite. For some diets, doctors prescribe drugs such as ephedrine to help suppress the appetite. Some dieters join a weight-loss group in their attempt to lose weight. Some of these groups, such as Overeaters Anonymous, are non-profit organisations. Others, such as Weight Watchers, are commercial concerns. Groups differ in their aims – some offer special menus, some provide their own brand of prepared food, and others focus mainly on providing emotional support and giving practical information.

Of course, there are also a large number of named weight-loss diets to choose from. The weight-loss diet book is a multimillion pound industry in its own right. These diets tend to go in and out of fashion, and are frequently promoted by celebrities, their creators, or both. Many of these diets – the Atkins Diet being a prime example – are controversial, in that the medical and scientific community becomes divided over how effective and healthy the diet actually is. Before starting one of these diets, the golden rule is to find out as much about it as possible. The internet is a valuable source of information, and your local GP can also advise you whether a particular diet is suitable for your needs.

V Vocabulary

1 Use a word in each gap to complete the phrasal verbs.

1 come ______________ (= regain consciousness)
2 cheer ______________ (= become happier)
3 come ______________ with (= fall ill with)
4 break ______________ (= appear suddenly in large numbers, of a disease)
5 pass ______________ (= faint)
6 get ______________ (= recover from)

2 Use a phrasal verb from exercise 1 in the correct form in each gap to complete the sentences.

1 The heat was too much for him and he ______________ ; he only ______________ when we carried him outside into the fresh air.
2 This illness first ______________ in China but it soon spread to the West.
3 Carol has ______________ the flu and she has to stay at home, so I sent her some flowers to ______________ her ______________ .
4 It's a simple operation and I am confident that you will soon ______________ it.

3 Choose the correct word or phrase to complete the text.

When I fell and cut my hand badly on some broken glass, I knew that it would need treatment. There was a health (1) **surgery / clinic** in town so I covered my hand to stop the bleeding and headed there. I was seen straight away by a doctor, who cleaned it up to prevent (2) **infection / prescription** and told me that I should see my own doctor in a few days. I hadn't been for a(n) (3) **operation / check-up** for years, so the doctor had a good look at me. Fortunately, he didn't find anything else wrong, so he gave me some (4) **tablets / injections** and told me to take one if the pain was bad. He also told me that I had to keep the hand clean in case of (5) **treatment / germs**.

4 If a sentence is correct, put a tick (✔). If it is incorrect, rewrite it correctly.

1 Almost any doctor you see will advise you give up smoking.

____

2 It's not like me be ill – I'm usually so healthy.

____

3 It's not worth take vitamins; just eat healthy food.

____

4 I'm a member of a gym but I don't always feel like going.

____

5 If you carry on working so hard, you're bound get ill.

____

6 You cannot force children eat vegetables.

____

7 My brother makes me go running with him – even in the rain!

____

8 My grandmother says there's no point to go to the doctor's.

____

Reading 2: vocabulary

1 Choose the correct word or phrase.

1 Which of these is *not* a doctor?
 a surgeon
 b specialist
 c GP
 d ward

2 Which of these is *not* done by a doctor?
 a looking at X-rays
 b spraining an ankle
 c taking your temperature
 d treating a patient

3 Which of these does *not* refer to an injury?
 a fracture
 b sprain
 c break
 d doubts

4 Which of these is *not* something wrong with you?
 a grin
 b infection
 c pain
 d sore throat

2 Choose the correct words to complete the sentences.

1 Being a doctor is very **commanding / demanding** and requires a lot of **variety / commitment**.
2 A new health **exercise / scheme** is being introduced which has been **injected / designed** by experts.
3 There are many different **aspects / cures** of alternative medicine but, for me, the most **fascinating / shattered** of all is aromatherapy.
4 **Committing / Treating** older people takes patience because they need a different kind of **care / feeling**.

E Use of English: exam practice

Read the text below. Use the word given in capitals at the end of some of the lines to form a word that fits in the gap in the same line. Write your answers IN CAPITAL LETTERS.

A DOCTOR'S LIFE

Being a doctor involves doing a huge (1) ______________ **VARY**
of different things. You may be involved in the
(2) ______________ of colds, or dealing with serious **TREAT**
injuries and diseases, or the giving of (3) ______________. **INJECT**
Even though many doctors try to stay emotionally
detached from their patients, it's hard to remain
(4) ______________ when you know that the patient **INVOLVE**
is counting on you to enable them to make a full
(5) ______________. Because of this, there is a lot **RECOVER**
of pressure. If you are a (6) ______________ or an **SURGERY**
anaesthetist, you have to deal with even greater
(7) ______________ because it really can be a matter of **RESPONSIBLE**
life and death when you are performing an
(8) ______________. Having said all that, doctors do get **OPERATE**
a huge amount of job (9) ______________ knowing that **SATISFY**
they are helping their patients recover. Also, the range
of (10) ______________ involved in a doctor's daily life **ACTIVE**
means that they rarely have time to feel bored.

G Grammar 2

1 Rewrite the sentences correctly using the words in brackets.

1 Could you make an appointment to see the doctor on Tuesday? (**me**)
2 Why don't you lend your book on health foods? (**him**)
3 The doctor wrote a prescription. (**me**)
4 They told that I might have to have a small operation. (**me**)
5 I cancelled my meeting with Helen in order go to the clinic. (**to**)
6 You should eat healthily so as avoid future problems. (**to**)

2 If a sentence is correct, put a tick (✔). If it is incorrect, rewrite it correctly.

1 She showed the test results me.
2 In order join the gym, you have to have this form signed by a doctor.
3 They gave to the young mother an information sheet on childhood illnesses.
4 You need to go out more in order to get some exercise.
5 Show to me exactly where you feel the pain.
6 I gave up junk food so to try to lose some weight.

E Use of English: exam practice

1 Read the text below and think of the word which best fits each gap. Use only one word in each gap. Write your answers IN CAPITAL LETTERS.

NATURALLY HEALTHY

Nature is something that we all too often take for (1) ______________ . Yet, in order (2) ______________ to become ill, we need to have regular contact with it – we need it (3) ______________ a regular basis. Imagine being kept in a room with no daylight and no greenery. Sounds (4) ______________ torture, doesn't it? Well, in fact it is. Just as animals suffer when they are kept in cages, we humans soon (5) ______________ ill in our own 'cages'.

What exactly we get from nature is not clear, so there may be several reasons why a walk in the countryside makes us (6) ______________ well. First of all, the oxygen from trees and plants gives (7) ______________ a lift as this oxygen fills the lungs, then the blood, and then goes straight to the brain, (8) ______________ us that familiar feeling of well-being. More difficult (9) ______________ explain is how the sense of smell works to make us happier. If something has a nice smell, like flowers or grass, (10) ______________ is likely that, apart from just being pleasant, it is (11) ______________ us some good as well. It is possible in many cases that the scents and aromas in nature remind us (12) ______________ our childhood – a time when all of us were younger, and most of us were fitter and healthier!

2 **Read the text below and decide which answer (A, B, C or D) best fits each gap.**

GET AHEAD OF THAT HEADACHE!

Millions of people (1) ______________ from headaches. It's a fact. What millions of people do not know is what causes them. Headaches are (2) ______________ with all kinds of health problems as well as your being under a lot of (3) ______________. Certain (4) ______________ like coffee can react badly with the chemical balance in our bodies and give us a headache as well.

The best thing to do if your head hurts is to (5) ______________ an aspirin, right? Wrong! You could be doing the worst thing possible because you are not (6) ______________ with the problem – only (7) ______________ the symptoms. And those people who think that painkillers can't do you any (8) ______________ are also wrong. Medical science has proved that, if we keep taking the tablets, they will soon (9) ______________ as a 'trigger' and, instead of curing your headache, they will (10) ______________ you worse.

So what do you do (11) ______________ your head starts to throb? Breathe deeply. It may be that you are not getting enough oxygen. Then, you could try massaging the side of your head with your fingers. And close your eyes. Often your eyes are very tired, and the best (12) ______________ for tiredness is sleep.

	A	B	C	D
1	**A** die	**B** pain	**C** ache	**D** suffer
2	**A** produced	**B** caused	**C** associated	**D** based
3	**A** stress	**B** worry	**C** fear	**D** anxiety
4	**A** materials	**B** substances	**C** vitamins	**D** drugs
5	**A** take	**B** drink	**C** eat	**D** put
6	**A** solving	**B** removing	**C** dealing	**D** treating
7	**A** re-living	**B** reducing	**C** resolving	**D** relieving
8	**A** badness	**B** harm	**C** negativity	**D** illness
9	**A** perform	**B** act	**C** look	**D** treat
10	**A** make	**B** do	**C** create	**D** diagnose
11	**A** should	**B** were	**C** if	**D** whether
12	**A** prescription	**B** check-up	**C** cure	**D** clinic

E Listening: exam practice

CD Track 11 You will hear people talking in five different situations. For questions 1–5, choose the best answer (A, B or C).

1 You hear a man talking. Why did he choose to become a nurse?
  A His mother used to be a nurse.
  B A nurse helped him in hospital.
  C He watched a programme on TV.

2 You hear a doctor talking. How does she feel about her work?
  A She would like more time with each patient.
  B She would like less paperwork.
  C She would like better equipment.

3 You hear a father talking to his daughter. Why is he talking to her?
  A to refuse permission
  B to give a warning
  C to make a suggestion

4 You hear a teenage girl talking about going to the dentist. How did she feel at the dentist's?
  A confident
  B uncomfortable
  C frightened

5 You hear a vet talking to a boy. Why has the boy brought his rabbit to the vet?
  A It isn't eating properly.
  B There's a problem with its eyes.
  C It doesn't have enough energy.

11

Learning

Reading 1: vocabulary

1 **Use a word from the box in each gap to complete the sentences.**

playground • break • undergraduate • extracurricular • report • scholarship

1 I wish I had more time for ______________________________ activities like music and sports.
2 Sebastian was awarded a ______________________________ so his parents didn't have to pay any school fees.
3 All the kids look forward to ______________________________ time, when they can meet their friends and relax for a bit in between classes.
4 We're going to get our end-of-term ______________________________ next week.
5 As soon as the bell rings, the ______________________________ fills with running and shouting children.
6 Being an ______________________________ is both fun and challenging, especially in the first year.

2 **Match each word or phrase 1–6 with a meaning a–f.**

1 be posted abroad ___
2 excel ___
3 distraction ___
4 agonise ___
5 fend for ___
6 show off ___

a worry a lot
b behave in a way designed to attract attention
c something that draws your attention away from what you are doing
d do extremely well at something
e be sent to do a job in a foreign country
f look after, take care of

3 **Use a word from the box to replace each word or phrase in bold.**

recollections • traumatic • aid • debate • bright • blossom

1 From an early age, Ruby appeared to be a very **intelligent** girl. ______________
2 My first **memories** of school are very happy ones indeed. ______________
3 We can **argue about** the subject for hours, but we'll still disagree. ______________
4 Mara struggled a bit in school, but I'm sure she'll **develop** at college. ______________
5 Good organisational skills are the best **support** to learning. ______________
6 Very few kids find living away from home **upsetting**. ______________

G Grammar 1

1 Use a form of the words in brackets in each gap to complete the sentences.

1 If you ______________ (**study**) more, you'd have a good chance of getting a scholarship.
2 Suppose you ______________ (**be**) accepted at both universities, which one would you choose?
3 I'd rather you ______________ (**not do**) disturb me when I'm studying.
4 It's high time I ______________ (**pass**) this exam!
5 If only Sam ______________ (**not show off**) so much!

2 Choose the correct word or phrase to complete the sentences.

1 I wish I **have / had** tried harder to do well in maths.
2 How I wish you **wouldn't / won't** make such a noise all the time!
3 I wish we **could / would** take the exam next week instead of tomorrow.
4 Sasha wishes she **hadn't failed / didn't fail** her French exam this year.
5 Adam really wishes he **wouldn't / didn't** have to do the summer course.

E Use of English: exam practice

Complete the second sentence so that it has a similar meaning to the first sentence, using the word given. Do not change the word given. You must use between two and five words, including the word given. Write the missing words IN CAPITAL LETTERS.

1 I have too much work to do so I can't go out with you tonight.
only
If ______________ so much work, I could go out with you tonight.

2 Please don't copy my answers!
rather
I ______________ copy my answers!

3 Daria needs to get a scholarship in order to go to that college.
if
Daria could go to that college ______________ a scholarship.

4 I don't like living so far from school.
closer
I wish ______________ school.

5 I regret not buying that book you recommended.
only
If ______________ that book you recommended.

6 You don't pay enough attention in class.
wish
I ______________ attention in class.

7 You'd better start revising for the exam!
time
It's ______________ revising for the exam.

8 Maybe my dream will come true and I'll go to Cambridge!
if
What ______________ true and I went to Cambridge!

E Reading: exam practice

You are going to read an article about modern education. For questions 1–8, choose the answer (A, B, C or D) which you think fits best according to the text.

The Changing Face of Education

Despite a rapidly changing world where technology and globalisation have had an impact on almost every possible corner of our lives, methods of education in the modern world haven't really been affected very much. In fact, the way young people learn in schools and colleges is remarkably similar to when free, compulsory education for all, was first introduced. But what if getting an education doesn't just mean getting up and going to a school or college building and sitting in a classroom reading books and listening to a teacher?

Although lessons are still held in classrooms, computers and technology have already started to play a major role in modern education. This role can only grow as the power of computer memory increases while the cost of computers drop. Computers can replace books, assist teaching, be used in testing and provide teachers with a plentiful supply of teaching resources. Though they are already an essential part of education, the day that they become the core tool for receiving an education cannot be very far away. How long before they replace classrooms?

Possibly not that long at all if colleges and universities are anything to go by. Many universities now offer online degree courses that are completed only over the internet.

This means that it doesn't matter where you are in the world, you can still have access to a university education without moving to the country the university is in. What would happen if schools offered the same learning opportunities too? Perhaps one of the main

1 In the first paragraph the writer says that education
A hasn't altered a great deal in recent decades.
B has been deeply affected by technology and globalisation.
C is exactly the same as when free education became available.
D no longer requires attending a school or college.

2 The writer believes that computers and technology in education will
A only increase when computers get cheaper.
B one day become essential.
C drastically change all aspects of learning.
D give teachers a lot of extra work.

3 The writer points out that online courses
A are now the main way to get a degree.
B need only a few lessons at the university.
C are the same all over the world.
D make it easier to get a university education.

4 The writer thinks online learning will
A never be available in schools.
B become more widespread in schools eventually.
C only ever be available for children in isolated areas.
D affect how children are looked after.

5 One advantage of the increasing use of technology in learning is that
A people of all ages will have greater access to education.
B young people won't have to choose between work or study.
C people would worry less about passing exams.
D older people will use the internet a lot more.

6 The word 'it' in line 30 refers to
A people's age.
B family.
C education.
D giving up work.

7 The writer believes some teachers may find it particularly difficult to
A get better training in the future.
B see anything positive in new teaching methods.
C accept that they won't come into personal contact with students.
D admit that technology is changing the world.

8 Overall the writer is
A critical of current teaching methods.
B sorry that old teaching methods will die out.
C angry about how slowly education is changing.
D enthusiastic about the use of technology in learning.

reasons why this type of learning hasn't taken off at school level, except in isolated areas, is because parents want their children to be looked after while they are at work. As the world of work changes, it might not be long before it stops being necessary for children physically to go to school.

Another benefit of getting away from traditional teaching methods and using technology more and more as an educational tool is that it means that education in the future won't just be something that is mainly associated with the young. There will be much more opportunity for lifelong learning. Imagine if, at any time of your life, you could just find the course you want to do on the internet and do it whenever it suited you. You wouldn't have to worry about giving up work or moving away from your family in order to study. Having so much greater choice over how people study will make **it** much more attractive to them, whatever their age. At the moment, one of the main stumbling blocks to change is the teachers who have been trained to teach using traditional methods. Some of them may find it hard to adapt to the kind of teaching where they need to give up books and the blackboard and embrace tablet computers, smartphones and social media as positive teaching tools. Even harder will be giving up on classrooms entirely and having little to no face-to-face contact with pupils or students. However, it's doubtful that any resistance to new ways of learning will last very long because there's just no getting away from the fact that the world is changing, technology is becoming more and more central to our daily lives both at home and at work. So, why would education be the only part of our lives that looks backwards to earlier times? In the end it won't. Education and learning methods will have to change in order to reflect the world and the lives we lead.

V Vocabulary

1 Choose the correct word to complete the sentences.

1 My aerobics **instructor / professor** is really great this term.
2 When you are at university, you will have several course **tutors / trainers**.
3 Dr Mathews is one of the most distinguished **teachers / professors** at the university today.
4 Simon works as an German **teacher / professor** at the local secondary school.
5 Alice is going to be a carpenter's **pupil /apprentice** for the next three years.
6 Joey Cicero is the new football **coach / teacher** at my school.
7 Julie will be a **trainee / training** nurse until her graduation next spring.

2 Use a word or phrase from the box in each gap to complete the sentences.

certificate • skill • licence • exam result • degree

1 Melanie's doing a __________ in ancient Greek at the University of Warwick at the moment.
2 Being able to use a computer is an extremely useful __________ .
3 I'm going to buy a second-hand car as soon as I get my driving __________ .
4 When Dawn finally got her __________ she framed it and hung it on the wall.
5 Our French teacher's going to give us our __________ tomorrow. I hope I've done well!

E Use of English: exam practice

1 Read the text below and decide which answer (A, B, C or D) best fits each gap.

Top Marks

Becky Davidson isn't one of those students who gets (1) __________ about exams. While many of her fellow students are having (2) __________ about whether they will (3) __________ or, worst of all, (4) __________ their exams, Becky is relishing the chance to realise her (5) __________ .'A lot of people just go to (6) __________ because of exam (7) __________ whereas I feel that a little pressure will help (8) __________ me and give me energy,' she says.'For me, the key is not to (9) __________ . Remember that what you're up (10)__________ is really just yourself. So try to enjoy it by being better than you ever were before.' Becky's advice is in many ways just good common (11) __________ and a useful (12) __________ for anyone who wants to do well in their exams.

	A	B	C	D
1	**A** shaky	**B** bashful	**C** anxious	**D** awkward
2	**A** ordeals	**B** misery	**C** distress	**D** nightmares
3	**A** pass	**B** take	**C** give	**D** sit
4	**A** omit	**B** fail	**C** neglect	**D** flop
5	**A** capacity	**B** potential	**C** possibility	**D** gift
6	**A** parts	**B** chunks	**C** fragments	**D** pieces
7	**A** stress	**B** burden	**C** tenses	**D** emphasis
8	**A** arouse	**B** persuade	**C** motivate	**D** disturb
9	**A** fear	**B** panic	**C** alarm	**D** scare
10	**A** beside	**B** opposed	**C** facing	**D** against
11	**A** reason	**B** sense	**C** feeling	**D** judgement
12	**A** action	**B** routine	**C** strategy	**D** procedure

Reading 2: vocabulary

1 Use a word from the box in the correct form in each gap to complete the text.

satisfaction • fulfil • arm • traumatise • minute • highlight

Some people wonder why, at the age of 32, I decided to go to university and get a degree. It wasn't a last (1) ______________ decision but something I'd thought about for a good few years. I knew that I would feel much more (2) ______________ if I went to study the subject I loved. It wasn't always easy. I felt self-conscious about being so much older than most students. But (3) ______________ with my books and lecture notes I soon managed to fit in. I wasn't as (4) ______________ by the experience as I had expected. Of the many (5) ______________ of my university life, the day I graduated was the best. I can't describe the sense of (6) ______________ I got from graduating at 35 years old!

2 Match each word or phrase1–6 with a meaning a–f.

1 unscrupulous ___
2 manageable ___
3 effectively ___
4 a mile off ___
5 past papers ___
6 factor in ___

a old exam papers
b easy to deal with
c include
d from far away
e dishonest / without principles
f in an efficient way

G Grammar 2

1 Find two unnecessary words in the sentences.

1 The group of girls who were sitting in the back of the library giggled quietly.
2 Many of the students who are graduating this year will go on to college.
3 Of all the students who are applying for a scholarship, you deserve to get it.
4 The books which are lying on the desk belong to Carol.

2 Use a word from the box in the correct form in each gap to complete the sentences.

open • realise • study • do • complete • try • pay

1 ______________ all through the night, I felt tired but confident for the next day's exam.
2 Students ______________ their third year at university often have to write a long essay.
3 ______________ unsuccessfully to figure out the homework on my own, I called a friend for help.
4 Imagine my shock on ______________ my bag and discovering it was someone else's!
5 ______________ a deposit already, I decided to attend the summer course after all.
6 ______________ from an early age that I only wanted to be a surgeon, I made sure I always did well at sciences at school.
7 ______________ all my homework, I went out with friends to see a movie.

3 Use one word to replace the words in bold in the sentences.

1 I've made a lot of good friends since **I came** to this school. ______________
2 **Because they heard** the bell, the students ran out into the playground. ______________
3 After **I had sat** at the computer for hours, I needed to take a walk. ______________
4 Despite **the fact that I was** told the exam was impossible, I passed first time. ______________
5 **Because I have** done a lot of research on this at university, I think I'm a good candidate for the job. ______________

E Use of English: exam practice

1 Read the text below and think of the word which best fits each gap. Use only one word in each gap. Write your answers IN CAPITAL LETTERS.

DIFFICULTIES OR DIFFERENCES?

There has (1) ______________ much debate about the expression 'learning difficulty' in recent years. While it is agreed (2) ______________ some children and adults (3) ______________ find it more difficult to learn (4) ______________ others, one wonders whether some individuals actually (5) ______________ difficulty learning, or if they just learn differently.

Research (6) ______________ shown, however, that the minds (7) ______________ dyslexics do in fact operate in a different way (8) ______________ those of non-dyslexic people. They show increased activity (9) ______________ response to certain things where non-dyslexic people don't, especially when dealing (10) ______________ graphics and design, (11) ______________ is why dyslexics often excel at the arts. Perhaps the difference then is (12) ______________ important than the difficulty!

2 **Read the text below. Use the word given at the end of some of the lines to form a word that fits in the gap in the same line. Write your answers IN CAPITAL LETTERS.**

TEACHING SATISFACTION

The professors, lecturers and other (1) ______________ like me,	**ACADEMY**
who work at our universities, are responsible for overseeing the	
(2) ______________ of the brightest people in the country. When I	**EDUCATE**
came to the (3) ______________ that I wanted a university career, I	**DECIDE**
felt it would be an opportunity to demonstrate my	
many (4) ______________ and I wanted to help pass on	**ABILITY**
(5) ______________ to other generations too. It's not as highly	**KNOW**
paid as some jobs but after much (6) ______________ I realised	**REFLECT**
that money, though a (7) ______________ necessity for everyone,	**PRACTICE**
was not the most important thing in my life. I get great personal	
satisfaction from ensuring that under my (8) ______________	**INSTRUCT**
hundreds of young people every year acquire the	
(9) ______________ they need to start them out in life with a	**QUALIFY**
realistic chance of being (10) ______________ in their own	**SUCCEED**
chosen careers.	

E Listening: exam practice

CD Track 12 **You will hear five different people talking about taking a driving test. For questions 1–5, choose from the list (A–F) the problem each person faced. Use the letters only once. There is one extra letter which you do not need to use.**

A getting confused about something	Speaker 1 ___
B hitting something	Speaker 2 ___
C using equipment	Speaker 3 ___
D not arriving on time	Speaker 4 ___
E having to deal with an emergency	Speaker 5 ___
F understanding someone	

12

The Law

Reading 1: vocabulary

1 Use a preposition in each gap to complete the phrases.

1 have a negative impact ______________
2 a direct link ______________
3 a rise ______________
4 a cause ______________ concern
5 to come out ______________ top
6 to be taken ______________ court
7 to stop someone ______________ doing something
8 to focus ______________
9 to concentrate ______________
10 to lead ______________

2 Use a phrase from exercise 1 in the correct form in each gap to complete the sentences.

1 There has been ______________ the number of young people committing crimes over the last six months.
2 We all know that smaller crimes often ______________ bigger ones.
3 The police arrested him and he ______________ .
4 If a friend of yours is about to break the law, you should try to ______________ it.
5 The problem of crime is ______________ .
6 Television violence ______________ young children.

3 Choose the correct word or phrase to complete the sentences.

1 He stole some money but he gave it back because he couldn't stand the feeling of **guilt / justice**.
2 The police **reflected / re-enacted** the crime to try to understand how it was done.
3 If you ever think about doing something illegal, just think about the **repercussions / coincidences**.
4 Cases of violence should be **punished / reported** to the police.
5 He said he had **stolen / robbed** the bank because he was desperate for money.

G Grammar 1

1 Match to make sentences.

1 Hardly had he put the phone down ___
2 No sooner had I stepped out of the door ___
3 At no time in my life ___
4 Under no circumstances ___
5 Not only had he been shoplifting ___
6 Little did I realise ___

a would I protect a friend who had committed a crime.
b but he had also stolen someone's credit card.
c when he heard the sound of police sirens.
d that the police were watching me.
e than I felt a hand on my shoulder.
f have I ever taken something that didn't belong to me.

2 **Use *have, do* or *be* in the correct form in each gap to complete the sentences. Use the words more than once.**

1 Little ______________ you realise how serious this is.
2 Scarcely ______________ I finished locking the shop when someone hit me from behind.
3 Not only ______________ criminals steal property, but they also cause a lot of damage.
4 Not until we got home ______________ we find out what had happened.
5 Under no circumstances ______________ you allowed to leave the building.
6 Most days, no sooner ______________ I got to my office than the phone starts to ring.
7 They cannot find the criminal, nor ______________ they able to say what time it happened.
8 At no time ______________ I ever suggested that you took my bag!

3 **Use a word or phrase from the box in each gap to complete the text.**

have I ever • did I realise • sooner had • did • nor • only • was • when • not • hardly

No (1) ______________ I left the house than I got a strange feeling that it was not going to be a normal day. Little (2) ______________ that it was going to lead to my arrest! As usual, I got off the bus a few streets from my office. Now, at no time in the past (3) ______________ walked the rest of the way to work past the shops, but that day I decided to vary my route. (4) ______________ had I turned the corner into the main shopping street (5) ______________ I noticed someone running towards me. I neither noticed the bag under his arm, (6) ______________ did I realise that it was the same as mine. (7) ______________ until he came right up to me and I saw the expression on his face (8) ______________ I understand that he had committed a crime. (9) ______________ after I had been pushed to the ground by two policemen (10) ______________ I able to fully understand the situation. All I kept thinking was that my boss was never going to believe me!

E Use of English: exam practice

Complete the second sentence so that it has a similar meaning to the first sentence, using the word given. Do not change the word given. You must use between two and five words, including the word given. Write the missing words IN CAPITAL LETTERS.

1 I got a message telling me he had been arrested as soon as I got home. **when**
Hardly ______________________________ I got a message telling me he had been arrested.
2 This is the best time to join the police force. **been**
Never ______________________________ time to join the police force.
3 I wouldn't steal money, no matter what happened. **would**
Under ______________________________ steal money.
4 You have absolutely no idea how serious this could have been. **realise**
Little ______________________________ how serious this could have been.
5 Straight after the news was my favourite crime series. **finished**
No sooner ______________________________ my favourite crime series came on.
6 I've never witnessed a crime. **time**
At ______________________________ ever witnessed a crime.
7 It's hardly ever necessary to put young offenders in prison. **is**
Rarely ______________________________ to put young offenders in prison.
8 We will not let you leave until we have finished our enquiries. **allowed**
Only after we have finished our enquiries ______________________________ leave.

E Reading: exam practice

You are going to read part of an interview where different people give their views on crime and the law. For questions 1–15, choose from the people (A–E). The people may be chosen more than once.

Which person

does a job for free?	1 ___
mentions the heartache of losing items you're emotionally attached to?	2 ___
helps people to reject a life of crime?	3 ___
was embarrassed about going to court?	4 ___
took on their job in order to contribute to society more?	5 ___
works with a large number of different organisations?	6 ___
doesn't think that crime has increased recently?	7 ___
hadn't been aware how much a particular crime can affect people?	8 ___
was angry about an intrusion into their personal life?	9 ___
believes there are times when prison is unavoidable for some crimes?	10 ___
wishes they could meet more ordinary people while working?	11 ___
mentions the satisfaction they get from the work they do?	12 ___
didn't believe that it was fair to be prosecuted for something?	13 ___
would like to spend less time working at their desk?	14 ___
mentions that a criminal had been caught many times before?	15 ___

A **John – Police officer**

I've been in the service for nearly 30 years. Lots of people think that crime is much worse nowadays than it was in the past. It's not actually true. What has changed is the types of crime. Now, it's antisocial behaviour that's on the rise, while serious violent crime is down. Police work itself has changed a lot too. We don't have as much contact with the local community and I think that is one of the reasons people don't have as much faith in the force as they used to. But government cuts mean we don't have the time to go out on the beat. Another problem is that I spend more time writing up reports than I do on actual police work. It can be very frustrating.

B **Alison – Magistrate**

In England and Wales magistrates deal with about 95% of all criminal cases. Scotland has a slightly different legal system to the rest of the UK, though. Anyone can volunteer to become a magistrate, but you do have to be able to show that you are of good character and have sound judgement. We don't get paid for doing it either, but we do get our expenses paid. I decided to become a magistrate to give something back to the community. I have to deal with a lot of different cases and some of them can be quite disturbing. I recently imprisoned a man who'd robbed and beaten an elderly couple. Although I try to avoid giving harsh sentences, sometimes it really is the only option, especially when violence is involved.

C **Cindy – Crime victim**

It's very upsetting when you walk into your home after it's been burgled. First of all, there's the mess. Everything is pulled out of drawers and cupboards and thrown on the floor. Then there's the distress when you find out what precious items have been taken. It's the sentimental value of personal items that's important, not their price tag. But perhaps worst of all is the anger you feel at having your home invaded by a stranger. I was lucky that the person who burgled my house was caught and I got most of my stolen property back. Most burglars are never caught. The man who burgled my house was a repeat offender and he'd only just got out of prison a couple of days before he burgled my home.

D **Dylan – Juvenile offender**

I was caught, along with a couple of friends, doing graffiti on the side of a building. We were charged with criminal damage and I got a fine from the youth court. It was an awful experience going to court. I felt really ashamed. Mainly because my parents were really upset about it. At first, I was angry about being taken to court because I didn't think that what we had done was criminal. It was art. But my dad took me to meet some people who had had their property damaged by graffiti and I realised that it can upset people and it costs them money to clean it up. I still think graffiti is art but I only do it now when I have permission.

E **Mark – Probation Officer**

I have various duties to perform as a probation officer including supervising people who have been let out of prison early on parole. It's my job to try and help them fit back into the community, find work and become useful, law-abiding citizens. I work with a lot of different people such as the police, social services and many charities. I have a very heavy workload as I have to deal with thousands of cases and each one is different. The work is very rewarding when you see someone turn their life around and you know you helped them do it. But it can be depressing sometimes, too, especially if someone reoffends and you have to send them back to prison.

V Vocabulary

1 Match the people to the definitions.

1 the accused ___
2 the judge ___
3 the jury ___
4 a solicitor ___
5 a witness ___
6 an offender ___
7 a convict ___

a the person who announces the verdict and passes sentence
b a person who gives advice about the law
c the twelve people who decide if someone is guilty or not guilty
d a criminal, someone who commits a crime
e the defendant, the person who has been taken to court
f a prisoner, someone serving a prison sentence
g someone who sees a crime being committed

2 Use a word from exercise 1 in the correct form in each gap to complete the sentences.

1 Young ____________ are often given fines instead of being sent to prison.
2 The ____________ asked the ____________ if they had reached their verdict.
3 I wanted to sell my house, so first I contacted my ____________ .
4 There were fears that a vital ____________ would not appear in court because he had been threatened.
5 Two policemen led the ____________ into the courtroom and some of the members of the public began shouting at him.

3 Use a phrasal verb from the box in the correct form in each gap to complete the sentences.

beat up • let off • get away with • go off • make off • break in

1 The judge decided that, because of the circumstances, he would ____________ him ____________ with a warning.
2 So far, no-one has claimed responsibility for the bomb that ____________ in the city centre last night.
3 Make sure you have a good lock on the back door so that it's difficult for thieves to ____________ .
4 The bank robbers ____________ with over €15,000 in cash.
5 'You'll never ____________ this!' the man shouted as the thief ran away.
6 The two men were sentenced to six months in prison because they had ____________ an innocent young man.

4 If a sentence is correct, put a tick (✓). If it is incorrect, rewrite it correctly.

1 When the young girl was accused to steal, she started to cry.

____

2 When they had collected enough evidence, the police finally charged the man of fraud.

____

3 Tim refused helping Stacey steal the sweets and ran home to tell his parents what she was planning to do.

____

4 Alan Halliwell, 27, was convicted for blackmail today at Manchester Crown Court.

____

5 Although the evidence was quite strong, the accused continued to deny having been involved in the crime.

____

6 Ray blamed his younger brother that he broke the window, but it wasn't really his fault.

____

Reading 2: vocabulary

1 Use a word from the box in each gap to complete the sentences.

theft • sentenced • goods • majority • fraction • slogans

1 It's my job to come up with imaginative advertising ____________ .
2 Organised criminal gangs are behind the trade in pirated ____________ .
3 He was charged with ____________ after he took money from the shop till.
4 He was ____________ to six months in prison for his part in the robbery.
5 The vast ____________ of people are law-abiding citizens.
6 You can buy copies of designer bags at a ____________ of the price.

2 Read the text below and decide which answer (A, B, C or D) best fits each gap.

An honest conman

Tom Keating was an art (1) ____________ with a difference. Tom hated the snobbery of art dealers and gallery owners so he decided to embarrass them by creating hundreds of (2) ____________ famous paintings. In contrast (3) ____________ other (4) ____________ painters, Tom left behind, in each of his paintings, a clue so that art restorers or real experts would know the work wasn't (5) ____________ . But no-one ever spotted the clues and he didn't (6) ____________ caught. Eventually, the large numbers of one particular painting on the art market (7) ____________ the suspicions of a dealer and Tom confessed to his (8) ____________ acts. If he hadn't admitted to the (9) ____________ he may never have been found out. Although what Tom did was (10) ____________ , he was never taken to court or (11) ____________ guilty of a crime. The fact that he came forward and confessed to the crime played a role in that. In the end honesty is always the best (12) ____________ .

	A	B	C	D
1	mimic	forger	copier	imitator
2	false	sham	fake	hoax
3	with	from	by	for
4	invalid	unreliable	lying	dishonest
5	real	genuine	true	actual
6	feel	be	get	have
7	started	aroused	provoked	stirred
8	impure	soiled	dirty	immoral
9	fraud	trick	lie	practice
10	banned	disallowed	illegal	disqualified
11	had	taken	found	claimed
12	action	policy	rule	procedure

G Grammar 2

1 Match the statements to the question tags.

1 You haven't seen my keys anywhere, ___
2 You won't get into any trouble, ___
3 You study law, ___
4 You've got an uncle who's a policeman, ___
5 He was in hiding for years, ___
6 He used to be in prison, ___
7 You don't want a police record, ___
8 He's the actor from that old detective series, ___

a haven't you?
b have you?
c isn't he?
d will you?
e wasn't he?
f do you?
g don't you?
h didn't he?

2 Complete the second sentence so that it has a similar meaning to the first. Use between two and five words, including the word given.

1 Everybody knows that he is a thief.
known
He ________________________ a thief.

2 They say the escaped criminal is carrying a gun.
believed
The escaped criminal ________________________ a gun.

3 Some people have said that it is a waste of money providing sports facilities in prisons.
said
It ________________________ providing sports facilities in prisons is a waste of money.

4 The police think the escaped man is hiding in the old farmhouse.
to
The escaped man ________________________ hiding in the old farmhouse.

5 Promise me you will not do it again.
do
You will ________________________ you?

6 Please tell me I don't look like the killer!
killer
I don't look ________________________ I?

E Use of English: exam practice

1 Read the text below and think of the word which best fits each gap. Use only one word in each gap. Write your answers IN CAPITAL LETTERS.

CRIME STATISTICS

Every year, statistics are released which show (1) ____________ has been happening in the country in terms of crime. But we should be suspicious (2) ____________ these statistics. They don't always tell us very much. If they have (3) ____________ prepared by the government, they will tend (4) ____________ emphasise the positive. In contrast, certain newspapers will (5) ____________ on the negative: the victims of crime, the violence, the dramatic rise.

Some statistics are interesting, however. It appears known, for example, that only 40% of all robberies (6) ______________ ever solved, compared to 90% of murders. That means that, (7) ______________ you be unfortunate enough to be robbed, the chances (8) ______________ ever recovering your property are small. Of course, it also means that one (9) ______________ ten killers is walking the streets right now. But take courage from the thought that, (10) ______________ you are murdered, the police (11) ______________ probably catch him (or her)!

And, as if you couldn't guess, most crimes involving vehicles and mobile phones are committed by people under 25. Finally, what is (12) ______________ most useless statistic of all? The fewest violent crimes – in fact, crimes of any kind – are committed by people in which age group? The over-60s!

2 **Read the text below. Use the word given in capitals at the end of some of the lines to form a word that fits in the gap in the same line. Write your answers IN CAPITAL LETTERS.**

CRIMINOLOGY

If you are considering becoming a (1) ______________ or thinking of	**LAW**
joining the police service, a knowledge of criminology is very useful.	
It includes learning how (2) ______________ is collected and how	**EVIDENT**
(3) ______________ are conducted, but it also involves learning	**TRY**
about the psychology of crime, how (4) ______________ think.	**CRIME**
This is very important in understanding why someone becomes an	
(5) ______________ and what makes them do what they do.	**OFFENCE**
Someone might commit (6) ______________ for example, for a	**THIEF**
number of reasons, ranging from poverty to seeking attention.	
Knowing what motivates a (7) ______________ or a	**ROB**
(8) ______________ might help in the prevention of crime and a	**MURDER**
reduction in (9) ______________ on the streets. The next time you	**VIOLENT**
hear about a crime on TV or in the newspapers, look at the	
(10) ______________ and ask yourself what led this person to a life	**ACCUSE**
of crime.	

E Listening: exam practice

CD Track 13 **You will hear a news report about a crime. For questions 1–5, complete the sentences.**

Joseph and Mary Carter live in a (1) ______________ house in Leeds.

The crime was initially discovered at around (2) ______________ in the morning.

The windows and doors had been installed (3) ______________ before.

Items such as the (4) ______________ in the living room were not stolen.

The police hope that the Carters' (5) ______________ might be able to provide some useful information.

Revision 2

E Reading: exam practice

You are going to read an extract from a novel. For questions 1–8, choose the answer (A, B, C or D) which you think fits best according to the text.

It was getting dark, and for the first time that day Gavin's thoughts turned to the people he'd had to leave behind. He pictured Lucy crying as she read his note, but he knew that she would understand. More than that, he knew that once she had recovered from the shock of his absence from her life, she would approve of his actions, would realise that he had had no choice, had had to escape.

Gavin then thought of Nathan, and wished he hadn't changed his mind at the last minute and stayed behind. Gavin ran through in his mind their final whispered conversation. Was there something else he could have said to persuade him? No, Nathan had made his decision and was firm. Gavin respected that, of course, but longed for Nathan to be with him. Together, they would have been able to share all the difficulties, give each other support and keep each other company. Now, Gavin had no-one to talk to and no-one to rely on except himself. That made everything doubly hard, but Gavin was sure of one thing – he didn't regret for a second his leaving.

Gavin thought also of the guards, and a smile spread across his face as he thought of them discovering that he was missing. He could see the panic on their faces, the lights coming on all over the building, the shouting, the checking that no-one else was missing too. Gavin hoped that no-one would be punished for his actions, but he knew the chances were that both Lucy and Nathan would suffer to some extent because of it. He prayed for them to be strong. He also prayed that Lucy had destroyed the note as soon as she'd finished reading it – as his p.s. at the bottom had requested. She was a smart and practical girl, so he had little doubt that she would do as he asked.

For the hundredth time that day, Gavin checked his money – \$87 in notes and \$2.50 in coins – and did the mental calculations he had been doing for several weeks. \$7 for food for six days is \$42. \$40 for bus tickets. That left \$7.50 for emergencies – and luxuries. In six days, he'd be in Memphis. Quite how Gavin was going to find Paul when he got there was something he hadn't worked out yet, but surely it wouldn't be impossible. Not knowing Paul's surname certainly made things harder, but Gavin had a strong feeling that luck would be on his side – for once. It had to be, otherwise he'd be out of money and out of options. 'Don't think about that now,' Gavin said to himself. 'Worry about the things you can control, and worry later about things that are going to happen later.'

Gavin looked at his watch and saw that it was just coming up to the hour. 'The local news'll be on in a minute,' he thought. 'Let's see if I'm being missed yet.' He got out his prize possession – a pocket-size battery-operated radio – and turned it on. A fire at a factory. Unemployment on the increase again. The opening of the new Museum of Science. Nothing about a teenage boy on the run. Gavin was astonished to feel a little disappointed. He realised part of him was actually looking forward to being famous, to being important, to being a hot topic of conversation on the lips of the residents of Carresville. He wasn't overly concerned that his photo would be on TV and on posters for miles around; the last photo the guards had taken of him was when he was thirteen. He'd changed a lot in the last two years and was fairly confident no-one would instantly recognise him. In fact, whenever he looked at that photo on his Centre ID Card, he didn't even recognise himself. Who was that innocent young boy looking back at him? Certainly not the Gavin of today.

1 Gavin believed that Lucy would
  A understand exactly where he had gone.
  B be too shocked by the news to think clearly.
  C be very upset by the news of his departure.
  D be glad that he was no longer around.

2 In their 'final whispered conversation' (line 6), Gavin
  A was unable to convince Nathan to stick to the original plan.
  B changed his mind and told Nathan he couldn't come with him.
  C was persuaded by Nathan that it was safer for Gavin to go alone.
  D did not try at all to persuade Nathan to change his mind.

3 What does the word 'That' in line 10 refer to?
  A Gavin's longing for Nathan to be with him
  B Gavin not having spoken to anyone
  C Gavin's ability to rely on himself
  D Gavin's being completely on his own

4 How did Gavin think the guards would react?
  A He didn't expect them to punish Nathan and Lucy for his actions.
  B He expected them to make life difficult for the friends he'd left behind.
  C He thought they would realise Nathan and Lucy had helped him.
  D He believed they would do nothing when they realised he was alone.

5 How certain was Gavin that Lucy had destroyed his note?
  A He was absolutely certain.
  B He was almost certain.
  C He was not very certain at all.
  D He was almost certain she hadn't.

6 What does the phrase 'for once' (line 24) suggest?
  A that Gavin knew he only needed to be lucky once in his life
  B that it was the first strong feeling he had had for a long time
  C that he rarely had strong feelings about how lucky he was
  D that Gavin believed that lucky things rarely happened to him

7 What was Gavin surprised about when he listened to the news?
  A that there was no mention of his escape
  B that he wished that he had been mentioned
  C that he had been expecting to hear about himself
  D that the news stories he heard had disappointed him

8 How did Gavin feel about his photo being shown on TV?
  A He wasn't worried because he knew it wasn't actually him in the photo.
  B He was extremely worried about it because people might recognise him.
  C He wasn't very worried because it would be difficult to identify him from it.
  D He was a little worried because the photo would also be on lots of posters.

E Use of English: exam practice

1 Read the text below and decide which answer (A, B, C or D) best fits each gap.

There are two things in the past decade that have had a huge effect on our social lives and what our culture (1) ______ for and they are both (2) ______ to each other. The first is the rise in social networking (3) ______ such sites as Facebook, and the second is the way smartphones have (4) ______ off in recent years. The (5) ______ majority of people now use one or the other, or both. It used to be (6) ______ that intimacy was the result of close personal relationships. But not anymore, now that social networking has taken (7) ______ much of our social lives. It's hard not to get involved in social networking when it's so easy to (8) ______ up an account. You provide the site (9) ______ a few details, click on a button and in a (10) ______ second you're in the network. It's hardly surprising, considering how popular they now are that these sites have really (11) ______ off for their owners, who have made very large (12) ______ from them.

	A	B	C	D
1	**A** looks	**B** represents	**C** sounds	**D** stands
2	**A** joined	**B** connected	**C** associated	**D** combined
3	**A** along	**B** via	**C** into	**D** inside
4	**A** taken	**B** given	**C** let	**D** set
5	**A** big	**B** huge	**C** vast	**D** immense
6	**A** repeated	**B** said	**C** spoken	**D** explained
7	**A** under	**B** round	**C** over	**D** down
8	**A** lay	**B** establish	**C** begin	**D** set
9	**A** with	**B** to	**C** for	**D** by
10	**A** divided	**B** split	**C** half	**D** fraction
11	**A** returned	**B** brought	**C** paid	**D** rewarded
12	**A** treasures	**B** riches	**C** possessions	**D** fortunes

2 Read the text below and think of the word which fits best in each gap. Use only one word in each gap. Write your answers IN CAPITAL LETTERS.

CHILD LABOUR IN THE PAST

When we hear people say that it must (1) ______ been hard living in the past, it's easy not to think too much about it. But for children (2) ______ lived in the nineteenth and early twentieth centuries, life was very unpleasant. For one thing, there were few schools, and (3) ______ that existed didn't offer much for the over-twelves. For the lucky ones, someone they knew would give (4) ______ a job and they could learn a trade. If they were fortunate enough (5) ______ have learned basic reading and writing skills, this could be in a large office. If not, however, it was usually in industry, (6) ______ conditions were dreadful. Children (7) ______ frequently injured by factory machinery or in mining accidents. The money was terrible, the hours were long, and if they (8) ______ a mistake, they (9) ______ the sack.

And let us not forget that, when people had their chimneys (10) ______, they sent young children up to do it, in (11) ______ of the fact that it was extremely dirty and unhealthy. Working part-time in the local shop doesn't sound so bad after all, (12) ______ it?

3 **Read the text below. Use the word given in capitals at the end of some of the lines to form a word that fits in the gap in the same line. Write your answers IN CAPITAL LETTERS.**

COMMUNITY SERVICE

When a (1) _______________ is caught and the judge or the magistrate has to	**CRIME**
choose a (2) _______________ , one of the options is sometimes community	**PUNISH**
service.	
A lot depends on the seriousness of the (3) _______________ committed, of	**OFFEND**
course, but, in general, community service is thought by many experts to be	
better than prison, which is not always (4) _______________ .	**BENEFIT**
There have been (5) _______________ cases of community service where	**COUNT**
the offender does some work, such as painting over graffiti or clearing up	
rubbish, which is (6) _______________ to the community but one scheme	**HELP**
seems to be an (7) _______________ on that – the work to be done by	**IMPROVE**
the offender is the (8) _______________ of the victim, and they meet in	**DECIDE**
person to talk about it. In experiments, both sides seem to benefit from this	
arrangement. If, say, a robber has a (9) _______________ with his victims, then	**DISCUSS**
it is not only (10) _______________ for the criminal, but it can also take away a	**EDUCATE**
lot of the victim's fear.	

4 **Complete the second sentence so that it has a similar meaning to the first sentence, using the word given. Do not change the word given. You must use between two and five words, including the word given. Write the missing words IN CAPITAL LETTERS.**

1 Phil said that he hadn't reported me to the manager.
reporting
Phil _______________________ to the manager.

2 You absolutely must not get on the wrong side of the police in this town.
should
Under no _______________________ on the wrong side of the police in this town.

3 Mrs Simmonds prefers it if nobody talks in class.
rather
Mrs Simmonds _______________________ in class.

4 The doctor is going to take out Jake's tonsils tomorrow.
taken
Jake is going to _______________________ tomorrow.

5 Do you think you could pass that dictionary to me?
would
Please _______________________ dictionary?

6 He said, 'Are you coming to football training tonight?'
whether
He asked _______________________ to football training that night.

7 He kept talking despite the fact that he knew I was studying.
even
He kept talking _______________________ he knew I was studying.

8 He said he would not cooperate with the police.
to
He _______________________ with the police.

E Listening: exam practice

CD Track 14 You will hear part of an interview with a linguist. For questions 1–5, choose the best answer (A, B or C).

1 What does Carol blame some journalists for?
  A not reporting important scientific discoveries
  B misrepresenting what scientists have said
  C not knowing any foreign languages

2 Carol says that it's obvious that
  A our DNA tells us which language to speak.
  B Japanese people have problems learning English.
  C where we live affects the language we speak.

3 According to Carol, the 'language gene' is
  A also found in apes and other animals.
  B what enables humans to use language.
  C definitely just one gene in our bodies.

4 Carol uses the example of making a question to show that
  A there are some things that no languages do.
  B Chinese and English are very different languages.
  C English is easier to learn than Chinese.

5 Which statement sums up Carol's view of language?
  A It's the regional differences that make humans special.
  B Human languages have more similarities than differences.
  C It would be better if we all learned one universal language.

E Writing: exam practice

1 You must answer this question.

You recently attended a course of lessons in a small language school in England. Now that you have returned, you have decided to write to the school, thanking them and making a few comments and suggestions. Read the original advertisement for the course and the notes you have made on it. Then write a letter to the language school owner giving your opinions and making your suggestions.

I really did!

COME AND IMPROVE YOUR ENGLISH IN ENGLAND!

We are offering courses for students of English at all levels.

Excellent idea – had to speak!

Maybe some classes should be smaller (20 in one class).

Discussion afterwards would be good.

- accommodation with local families
- small classes
- extensive use of video
- qualified teachers
- frequent trips
- all materials provided

Write a letter in 120–150 words. You must use grammatically correct sentences with appropriate spelling and punctuation in a style appropriate for the situation. Do not write any addresses.

Write an answer to one of the questions 2–4 in this part. Write your answer in 120–180 words in an appropriate style for the situation.

2 *You have had a discussion in class on the subject of health. Now, your teacher has asked you to write an essay giving your opinions on the following statement:*

Sport and exercise give you more than just a healthy body.

Write your essay.

3 *You recently saw this advertisement in your school magazine and have decided to apply.*

VOLUNTEERS NEEDED

The charity Action Now needs your skills – whatever they are. Come and volunteer for some of the work we do. You could be working with disabled people, children with learning difficulties or young offenders.

Whatever you do, you can make a difference to people's lives and gain valuable experience. Send a letter of application, telling us what you think you would be good at and why.

Write your letter of application to Action Now. Do not write any addresses.

4 *An international student magazine is running a series of articles called 'Crime and Punishment around the World'. You have been asked to write an article on the situation in your country, including details about the police and the law, and saying what happens to offenders.*

Write your article.

Speaking

1 Relationships

1 Make questions from the jumbled words.

1 still are education in you full-time both?

____

2 the what future for are plans your?

____

3 spare you what like do your time kind doing things in of?

____

4 you how there been long living have?

____

5 leave want do what school you to when you do?

____

6 you English how studying have long been?

____

2 Complete the dialogue using the words in the box.

there • like • where • do • it • from • what • both • year • great another • sure • know • one • definitely • decided

Interlocutor: (1) ______________ are you from?
Candidate A: I'm from Stockholm. I've lived (2) ______________ all my life.
Interlocutor: Do you (3) ______________ living there?
Candidate A: Yes, I (4) ______________ . It's an exciting city.
Interlocutor: And (5) ______________ about you? Where are you from?
Candidate B: I'm (6) ______________ Malmo. It's a big city in southern Sweden.
Interlocutor: What's (7) ______________ like living there?
Candidate B: It's (8) ______________ . Malmo is a very beautiful city.
Interlocutor: Are you (9) ______________ still at school?
Candidate A: I'm in my final (10) ______________ at high school.
Candidate B: I've still got (11) ______________ two years to go before I finish school.
Interlocutor: Do you (12) ______________ what you want to do when you leave school?
Candidate A: I'm not (13) ______________ . I haven't (14) ______________ yet. But (15) ______________ of my ambitions is to travel.
Candidate B: I (16) ______________ want to help people. So, I'm thinking of training to be a nurse.

2 Travelling

1 Each of the words in bold is in the wrong sentence. Write the correct word on the line.

1 You might **bored** an experienced guide to show you around. ______________

2 On holiday, you can get **nerves** from your daily routine. ______________

3 You could get **away** if you just do the same things every day. ______________

4 If the beaches are very crowded it could get on your **need**. ______________

5 Doing watersports is exciting **although** just lying on a beach is dull. ______________

6 I like sightseeing, **whereas** I would prefer to do more exciting activities. ______________

2 Choose the correct word to complete the monologue.

In the (1) **first / begin** picture I can see some people enjoying themselves doing watersports. In the (2) **another / other** one the person is hiking in the countryside. (3) **Two / Both** pictures show people doing healthy activities. (4) **Another / Other** similarity is that they both show outdoor activities. One key (5) **differ / difference** is that watersports can be expensive to do (6) **because / whereas** walking in the countryside doesn't cost a lot of money. Another (7) **way / one** in which they (8) **differ / different** is that watersports can be dangerous sometimes too. (9) **In / On** the whole, walking is quite safe, unless you get lost. Myself, I think I would go (10) **on / to** a hiking holiday as it's a really good way to enjoy the countryside. As (11) **long / far** as I'm concerned, I'd like to spend more time appreciating the natural world. I think a hiking holiday is the perfect way to get (12) **out / away** from our daily routines in towns and cities.

3 Technology

1 Complete the dialogue using the words in the box.

sum • fine • completely • would • about • what • agree • sure • point • like • say

Becky: So, what equipment shall we get for the youth club? (1) ______________ you like me to begin?

Gavin: Yes, that would be (2) ______________ .

Becky: OK. (3) ______________ do you think about getting the fridge? It would be useful because the one we have is quite old now.

Gavin: I'm not (4) ______________ that's a good idea. The old one is fine. I'd (5) ______________ to suggest the games console since I think everyone would enjoy using it.

Becky: You have a (6) ______________ , but I think people play games enough when they're at home. How (7) ______________ getting a video camera? It would be useful as we could video the activities we do at the youth club.

Gavin: I (8) ______________ to a certain extent but I'm not sure if everyone would be interested. I'd (9) ______________ that a DVD player would be more useful. We could show films and documentaries.

Becky: I (10) ______________ agree. That's a very good idea. Perhaps we could get the flat screen TV as well. It would be much better for showing films.

Gavin: Absolutely. So do we agree on our choices then?

Becky: Yes. To (11) ______________ up, we've chosen the TV and DVD player so that we can show films and documentaries at the club.

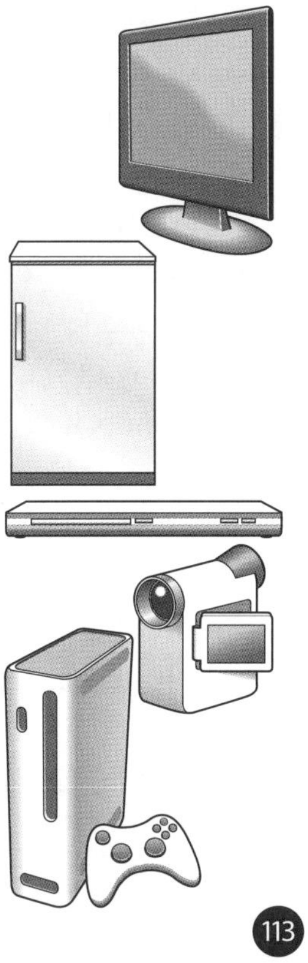

2 Match the questions 1–5 with their answers (a–e).

1 How do you think the world will change in the future? ____
2 What technological advances do you think you will see in your lifetime? ____
3 Do you think we rely too much on technology? ____
4 Do you think technology has made your life easier? ____
5 If you were an inventor, what would you invent? ____

a I suppose we do really. I don't think we would know how to survive without it.
b To be honest, I haven't thought about it much but I think the world will be a very different place.
c Well, I think I would want to make a car that could fly and travel on water.
d I think the main one will be with computers. I think they'll be capable of doing almost everything soon.
e That's an interesting question. Yes, to some extent, but I suppose in some ways it makes my life more complicated.

4 Money

1 Make questions from the jumbled words. Then match them with their responses (a–e).

1 things internet what the do on buy kind people of? ____________________ ____
2 feel how shops about small do in shopping you? ____________________ ____
3 of what supermarkets shopping are large advantages at the? ____________________ ____
4 anything have market at you street bought ever a? ____________________ ____
5 shopping what the of are disadvantages internet the on? ____________________ ____

a There are lots but mainly the fact that they have such a wide variety of goods.
b One problem is that you can't see the things you want before you buy them.
c You can buy almost anything at all online these days from food to musical instruments.
d Yes, I have. I go to one on Sundays to get CDs and DVDs.
e To be honest, I don't use them very much because they're often more expensive than large shops.

2 Complete the monologue using the words and phrases in the box.

while • as • as for • both • the second • on the other • in the first • another point • on the one

(1) ______________ pictures show different ways of shopping. (2) ______________ picture people are shopping at a mall. This is the modern way to shop nowadays. (3) ______________ picture shows a high street with lots of small shops. This isn't (4) ______________ popular a way to shop as malls are nowadays. (5) ______________ which way I prefer to shop, it depends on what I want to buy. (6) ______________ hand, malls are more convenient because you can find everything in one place. (7) ______________ hand, small high street shops have more character. (8) ______________ I'd like to make is that small shops are often more helpful and give a better service, (9) ______________ malls can be a bit unfriendly.

5 Leisure

1 Choose the correct word to complete the dialogue.

Simon: Right. I'd (1) **tell / say** that the tent is definitely one of the most useful things that we need.

Lily: Absolutely, and would you agree that the hunting knife would probably be (2) **extreme / extremely** useful too?

Simon: Definitely. The sun cream (3) **might / must** be useful, as well, because we'll be outdoors a lot.

Lily: I (4) **part / partly** agree with you but I'm not certain we'll really need it. It'll probably rain.

Simon: (5) **How / What** do you think about the mobile phone? I think it could be a good idea in case of an emergency.

Lily: You're right about that. But I'm not (6) **certain / definite** we'd need the laptop.

Simon: Me neither. It wouldn't be very useful at all. I think the barbecue could (7) **be / being** very useful, though. It's perfect for cooking when camping.

Lily: I agree to a certain (8) **extend / extent**, but it's quite big. Perhaps it would be better just to take a frying pan for quick, easy meals.

Simon: I see what you mean. But barbecues are fun. I'd (9) **put / suggest** that we get rid of the umbrella, though. It's too big and I don't think we'll need it.

Lily: I agree with you about that. It isn't something we need. So which do you think we (10) **shall / should** choose to leave behind?

Simon: (11) **Let's / Let** leave the umbrella and the laptop behind.

Lily: I agree we can do (12) **with / without** them.

2 Match the questions 1–5 with their answers (a–e).

1 Why does camping appeal to so many people? ___
2 Would you enjoy going camping with your friends? ___
3 Is camping suitable for families and older people? ___
4 What are the disadvantages of going camping? ___
5 Is camping bad for the environment? ___

a I don't see why it shouldn't be. As long as you're well organised, anyone can enjoy it.
b If you ask me, there's no reason why it should be, as long as people respect the environment when they go camping.
c Personally, I'd love to. I think it's a great way to go on holiday.
d Well, it can be a bit miserable to do if the weather is really bad.
e To my mind, it's because it's a chance to do something different and it's cheap too.

6 Nature

1 Each of the words in bold is in the wrong sentence. Write the correct word on the line.

1 It seems to **I'm** that deforestation is leading to mass extinction of species. ____________
2 As far as **me** concerned, we need to find alternative sources of energy. ____________
3 In my **mind**, air pollution is a very serious threat to our health. ____________
4 If you **view** me, not enough is being done to protect marine life. ____________
5 To my **opinion,** people are not doing enough to recycle their waste. ____________
6 In my **ask**, everyone should use public transport much more than they do. ____________

2 Complete the monologue using the words in the box.

it • no • to • of • similarity • my • in • result • if • concerned • shows • say

(1) ______________ begin with, the first picture is a view (2) ______________ a city that has very bad air pollution. (3) ______________ my opinion this is the (4) ______________ of too much traffic as well as industries polluting the atmosphere. The second picture (5) ______________ the countryside covered in litter. I'd (6) ______________ this is because of people not having any respect for the environment. In fact, this is one (7) ______________ between the pictures. (8) ______________ you ask me, both air pollution and litter in the countryside are problems caused by people being selfish. As far as I'm (9) ______________ , the key difference between the pictures is how serious each form of pollution is. To (10) ______________ mind, although litter is a serious problem, it's not as big a threat as air pollution. (11) ______________ seems to me that air pollution is worse because it's a threat to everyone's health. There's (12) ______________ doubt that everyone needs clean air to breathe.

7 Sport

1 Complete the sentences using the words in the box.

ambitions • enjoy • used • much • favourite

1 One of my ______________ sports is tennis.
2 I ______________ to like tennis but now I don't.
3 I don't have ______________ free time but when I do, I like playing basketball.
4 One of my ______________ is to win a swimming trophy.
5 I ______________ watching lots of sports at the weekend.

2 Match the questions 1–5 with their answers (a–e).

1 What do you think of extreme sports?
2 Do you prefer team or individual sports?
3 What do you like doing in your free time?
4 Have you tried any unusual sports?
5 What are the sports facilities in your area like?

a I enjoy doing all sorts of activities, including sport
b On the whole, they could be better because I think they're too expensive.
c As far as I'm concerned, they're not for me, as they're too dangerous.
d I prefer sports where people work together as a team.
e No, but I'd love to try bicycle polo one day.

8 Communication

1 Complete the dialogue using the words in the box.

about • suggest • afraid • would • say • example • true • sure • be • ask • partly • my

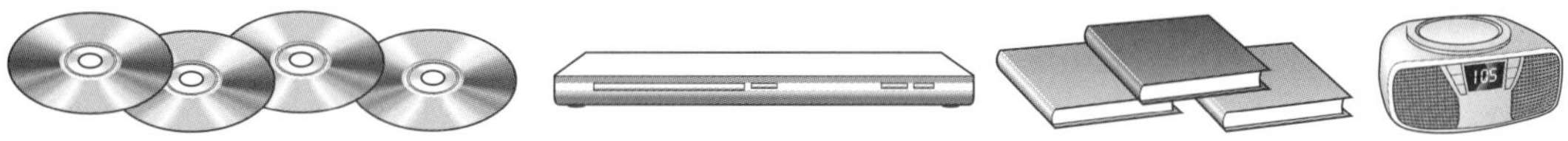

Leah: To begin, I'd like to (1) ________ the TV and DVD player. I think they're very useful for learning English because the students (2) ________ enjoy watching films or documentaries.

Paul: I (3) ________ agree with you as students definitely enjoy watching films and programmes but I don't think they really learn much. How (4) ________ the books? I think they're much better to learn English with and students always need to practise their grammar.

Leah: I'm (5) ________ I have to disagree. We use books all the time and they're a very old-fashioned way to learn English nowadays. I'd (6) ________ that the CD player and CDs are better because listening is one of the hardest parts of learning English. It would (7) ________ good practice.

Paul: I'm not (8) ________ I agree. To (9) ________ mind, they're also a bit old-fashioned. If you (10) ________ me, a computer is better because you can use it in so many different ways. You can watch videos or play interactive games on the internet, for (11) ________ .

Leah: That's (12) ________ . I completely agree that it is a good choice.

2 Make questions from the jumbled words.

1 people have do a young the on good media influence?
2 with do keep the you news to try up to date?
3 in images are the violent shown too media many?
4 the is what get the do news best to think way you?
5 the to in would media career you a like have?
6 we shown do are should programmes you certain control time think what?

9 Work

1 Each of the words in bold is in the wrong sentence. Write the correct word on the line.

1 **On** the picture, there's a nurse talking to a patient. ________
2 Another **way** difference is that media jobs are much better paid. ________
3 **In** the one hand, a career in nursing is very rewarding. ________
4 The first **prefer** I'd like to make is that both jobs can be stressful. ________
5 Another **key** in which they differ is that nurses have to wear a uniform. ________
6 As for which I would **point**, I think a media career would be fascinating. ________

2 Complete the monologue using the words in the box.

of • whereas • similarity • shows • both • go • although • one • another • definitely • with • seems • make • like

To begin (1) ________ , the first picture is (2) ________ a very nice modern office full of modern furniture. It's light and spacious and it looks (3) ________ a pleasant place to work. The other picture (4) ________ a tour guide taking people round the sights in a city. I can't quite (5) ________ out where they are though. (6) ________ of the main differences between the two jobs is that a tour guide often works outdoors (7) ________ office workers are indoors all day. (8) ________ point I'd like to make is that tour guides get to meet lots of different people every day. One (9) ________ between the jobs, though, is that they (10) ________ have long working hours. (11) ________ I think working in an office might be better paid, I think I would (12) ________ for working as tour guide as it (13) ________ a more exciting job. I would (14) ________ enjoy going to museums and galleries as part of a job, too.

10 Health

1 Choose the correct word to complete the dialogue.

Tina: Would you (1) **like / want** me to begin?

Mark: That (2) **could / would** be fine.

Tina: Well, I'd like to (3) **say / add** that I don't think doing sport is unhealthy even if people do get injured sometimes.

Mark: I (4) **would / completely** agree with you. There are definitely more advantages than disadvantages to sport. (5) **What / Think** about watching too much TV? That's very unhealthy.

Tina: I agree to a (6) **certain / total** extent. But I think it's something parents complain about rather than being a real problem. Everyone needs to relax. Listening to very loud music is (7) **much / more** worse.

Mark: In a (8) **part / way**, you're right. (9) **But / So** don't you think eating sugary fatty foods is worse? (10) **Lots / Many** of teenagers have weight problems nowadays.

Tina: You (11) **make / have** a point, although I think everyone knows it's unhealthy. I'd (12) **suggest / ask** it's more important to talk about the dangers of air pollution in the city.

Mark: I'm (13) **afraid / sure** I have to disagree because not everyone lives in a big city. I think unhealthy eating affects everyone.

Tina: You're (14) **true / right** I suppose. Let's choose that for our cover, then.

2 Match the questions 1–5 with their answers (a–e).

1 Do people worry too much about their health these days?
2 Do you think you have a healthy lifestyle?
3 Do you think teenagers learn enough about how to stay healthy?
4 What advice would you give someone who wanted to improve their diet?
5 Do you think people were healthier in the past?

a As far as I'm concerned, they don't know enough and that's bad, because it's important.
b I would explain how much better they would feel if they cut out fatty foods.
c I think it would be better if I exercised more.
d I'm sure they were because people used to walk a lot more and eat more fresh foods.
e I don't think so because most people don't seem to think about it at all.

11 Learning

1 Match the beginnings of the sentences 1–5 with their endings (a–e).

1 This is a picture
2 Another way in which they differ
3 I'm not absolutely sure,
4 I can't quite make
5 As for which I would

a is that they're enjoying the lesson in the first picture but not in the second.
b prefer, I think it's better to learn by actually doing things.
c out what kind of lesson it is.
d of a driving lesson.
e but it looks like a group of soldiers with some kind of map.

2 Complete the monologue using the words in the box.

other • much • tell • such • suppose • worth • although • ask • quite personally • first • though • have • sometimes • seem • hand

As far as I can (1) ________________, both pictures are showing different kinds of ways to learn. The (2) ________________ one shows children in an art lesson. They (3) ________________ to be very involved in what they're doing. In the (4) ________________ one, they are in a classroom and writing down information from the board. One point (5) ________________ mentioning is that in this picture they don't look as (6) ________________ they are enjoying it very much. I (7) ________________ it's not (8) ________________ as interesting as doing something with your hands. On the other (9) ________________, if the teacher is good it doesn't make (10) ________________ of a difference.
(11) ________________, I think that both types of learning are valuable.
(12) ________________ it's better to learn by doing things with your hands
(13) ________________ as in an art lesson; at other times you need to use your mind more. If you were to (14) ________________ me which I prefer, I'd
(15) ________________ to say the art lesson because I'm a creative person,
(16) ________________ I think traditional learning is important too.

12 The Law

1 Choose the correct word to complete the dialogue.

Dave: Is it (1) **good / OK** if I start?
Bella: I don't (2) **mind / think** at all.
Dave: Let me (3) **ask / see**. I think it would be a good idea if the article mentioned that you (4) **had / should** always lock your door.
Bella: I'd agree (5) **with / for** that. But what about (6) **recommend / recommending** that you should have bars on the window?
Dave: I'm not (7) **agree / sure** about that. Who wants to live as though they're in a prison?
Bella: (8) **Good / True** point. One possibility is having a 'beware of the dog' sign to put off burglars.
Dave: You have (9) **one / a** point, although it might not work if you don't actually have a dog.
Bella: That's true. (10) **How / What** do you think about neighbourhood watch schemes, where people patrol the streets?
Dave: I'm (11) **certain / afraid** I think it's a terrible idea. People shouldn't take the law into their own hands.
Bella: (12) **Another / Further** idea is warning people about looking after their bags or wallets as there are a lot of pickpockets about.
Dave: (13) **Possibly / Absolutely**. I think that's an excellent idea.
Bella: So, which two do you think we (14) **would / should** choose, then?
Dave: Let's (15) **be / go** for talking about keeping doors locked and watching your personal property.

2 Make questions from the jumbled words.

1 reasons what people main commit are the crimes?
2 to what be like do in it's prison think you?
3 punishment prison for do right most you crimes believe the is?
4 a area do your serious in you crime problem have with?
5 of can crime any you prevent other to think ways?

Answer key

Unit 1
Relationships

Reading 1

Exercise 1
1 g 2 h 3 e 4 a 5 b 6 d
7 c 8 f

Exercise 2
1 hurtful
2 perfectly balanced
3 saying
4 in common
5 rough patch
6 argument
7 annoy
8 anger

Exercise 3
1 a 2 b 3 a

Use of English: exam practice

1 WHICH / THAT
2 WITH
3 THEM
4 THEIR
5 TO
6 A / ANY / EACH
7 WITH / TO
8 WILL
9 FOR
10 HAVING
11 TO
12 WAS

Reading: exam practice

1 F 2 H 3 C 4 A 5 G 6 D 7 B

Vocabulary

Exercise 1
1 boring
2 relaxing
3 frightened
4 excited
5 tiring
6 annoying
7 interested

Exercise 2
1 rudely
2 appearance
3 nervously
4 relatives / relations
5 befriended
6 jealousy

Exercise 3
1 e 2 c 3 d 4 g 5 f 6 b 7 a

Exercise 4
1 nervous
2 funny
3 alone
4 selfish
5 polite
6 lonely
7 kind
8 honest

Reading 2

Exercise 1
1 c 2 e 3 f 4 a 5 b 6 d

Use of English: exam practice

1 A 2 C 3 C 4 D 5 B 6 D
7 B 8 A 9 D 10 B 11 A 12 A

Grammar 2

Exercise 1
1 have
2 had
3 had
4 had
5 hasn't
6 had
7 have
8 I've

Exercise 2
1 has been
2 had just moved
3 Have you ever had
4 had had
5 have just broken up
6 had only played

Use of English: exam practice

Exercise 1
1 ACTING
2 EXCITING
3 TALENTED
4 ATTRACTIVE
5 INTERESTING
6 DIFFERENT
7 QUALIFICATION
8 KNOWLEDGE
9 TIRING
10 DISAPPOINTMENTS

Exercise 2
1 TO RECOVER FROM
2 HAVE BEEN MARRIED SINCE
3 HAS BEEN ACTING FOR
4 WAS RAISED BY
5 HAVE PUT UP WITH
6 ME TO SORT OUT
7 HAVE ALREADY TRIED
8 HAD JUST TAKEN

Listening: exam practice

1 A 2 B 3 A 4 A 5 C

Unit 2
Travelling

Reading 1

Exercise 1
1 crackling
2 secluded
3 freedom
4 checked
5 swears

Exercise 2
1 excitement / ultimate / get bored
2 itching to / adventure / saddle / trails / tracked / streams
3 cabin / porch / valley
4 enjoy yourself / sheer / keep you busy

Grammar 1

Exercise 1
1 am driving
2 was packing
3 have been sitting
4 is already planning
5 was staying
6 had been lying

Exercise 2
1 were driving
2 are staying
3 had been travelling
4 have been looking
5 were you doing
6 went

Exercise 3
1 have been travelling
2 have been trying
3 have been resting
4 am leaving
5 have been doing / are doing
6 was sitting
7 were watching / watched
8 wanted / had wanted
9 had
10 am doing
11 try / am trying
12 haven't paid
13 am relying / have been relying / rely
14 were travelling / travelled

Exercise 4
were promising – had promised
had been leaving – were leaving
looked forward – was looking forward
is calling – had been calling
was making – made / had made

Reading: exam practice

1 C 2 B 3 A 4 C 5 D 6 C
7 B 8 D

Vocabulary

Exercise 1
1 c 2 b 3 d

Exercise 2
1 back
2 off
3 up
4 off
5 in
6 down

Exercise 3
1 business
2 inhabitants
3 broaden
4 trip
5 hotel
6 time

Use of English: exam practice

1 D 2 A 3 A 4 C 5 B 6 D
7 B 8 C 9 A 10 A 11 A 12 C

Reading 2

Exercise 1
1 a 2 c 3 c 4 b 5 a 6 b

Exercise 2
1 region
2 bound
3 carved
4 Getting
5 sled
6 festival

Grammar 2

Exercise 1
1 would
2 too
3 so
4 such
5 enough
6 used

Exercise 2
1 I love being on holiday but I am not used to having so much free time.
2 The tickets were too expensive so I couldn't go.
3 It was such a long and tiring journey that I was asleep when we arrived.
4 When we were there on holiday, I thought New Zealand was very / really / extremely interesting.
5 ✔
6 When I was very young, we used to live in Portugal.
7 ✔
8 My sister is not old enough, so she'll have to wait until next year.

Use of English: exam practice

Exercise 1
1 PREPARATIONS
2 NEAREST
3 OPTIONS
4 CATERING
5 LOCATION
6 PACKAGE
7 OUTDOOR
8 ACTIVITIES
9 SURVIVAL
10 ACHIEVEMENT

Exercise 2
1 HAVE BEEN GOING ABROAD SINCE
2 SUCH AN EXPENSIVE HOLIDAY
3 SEE HIM OFF
4 NOT OLD ENOUGH
5 USED TO SPEND
6 THE HOLIDAY OF A LIFETIME
7 INCREASINGLY POPULAR DESTINATION
8 GOT ON SO

Listening: exam practice

1 1829
2 prisoners (from Britain) / British prisoners
3 go surfing / surf
4 modern art
5 basketball

Unit 3
Technology

Reading 1

Exercise 1

1 mobile device
2 apps
3 download
4 handy
5 notify
6 gadgets

Exercise 2

1 voice recognition technology
2 monitor
3 search engine
4 take pride in
5 predictive text
6 unfolding

Grammar 1

Exercise 1

Students should have ticked 1, 4, 5, 7 and 8

Exercise 2

1 a 2 a 3 c 4 b

Exercise 3

1 all computers will be / all computers are going to be
2 I am going to study / I will study / I shall study
3 Shall I help
4 Will Chris really go / Is Chris really going / Is Chris really going to go
5 don't you talk / aren't you going to talk / won't you talk
6 people will communicate / people are going to communicate

Exercise 4

Students' own answers, based on the information provided.

Reading: exam practice

1 F 2 C 3 A 4 G 5 H 6 E 7 B

Vocabulary

Exercise 1

1 c 2 e 3 b 4 a 5 d

Exercise 2

1 have broken down
2 cut off
3 get through
4 look into
5 came up with
6 (had) put in

Exercise 3

1 achievement
2 beneficial
3 creative
4 developments
5 inventor
6 solution

Exercise 4

1 discovered
2 invented
3 research
4 investigation
5 portable
6 tools

Reading 2

Exercise 1

1 debt
2 brainwave
3 emigrate
4 figured out
5 sealed
6 gradually

Use of English: exam practice

1 B 2 D 3 C 4 B 5 A 6 D
7 C 8 C 9 A 10 B 11 A 12 B

Grammar 2

Exercise 1

1 the
2 a
3 the
4 –
5 –
6 the
7 the
8 the
9 a
10 –

Exercise 2

As __ teenagers are particularly open to __ new technology, companies that target this market are being advised to use the internet not only as a way to communicate their message to teens, but also to hear back from them. For __ instance, a recent consumer survey of teenagers' online behaviour conducted by the global research firm Jupiter MMXI emphasises how __ teenagers are 'spreading the word'. Almost __ forty per cent said that they shared __ information they had found on the net several times a week. Indeed, the primary reason most teenagers log on is to communicate with __ people of their age group. Throughout __ Europe, chat and email services feature among the most popular online destinations.

Exercise 3
1 know
2 buy
3 leave
4 ends
5 I'm going
6 grows
7 has listened

Use of English: exam practice

Exercise 1
1 INVENTOR
2 DISCOVERED
3 REVOLUTIONARY
4 CREATIVE
5 SCIENTIST
6 SOLUTIONS
7 PRODUCTS
8 BENEFICIAL
9 DEVELOPMENT(S)
10 ACHIEVEMENTS

Exercise 2
1 BREAKS DOWN
2 FIGURE OUT HOW TO
3 TAKE (IT) FOR GRANTED
4 BEFORE YOU TURN OFF
5 AS SOON AS SHE GETS
6 WHILE I'M WORKING
7 FOUND OUT WHO THE INVENTOR
8 COME UP WITH

Listening: exam practice
1 A 2 F 3 D 4 C 5 B

Unit 4
Money

Reading 1

Exercise 1
1 well
2 poverty
3 fortune
4 invest
5 for
6 business

Exercise 2
1 to go for it
2 to be well off
3 to make a fortune
4 to live in poverty
5 to go into business
6 to invest money

Exercise 3
1 dedication
2 savings
3 clients
4 cheap
5 makes
6 run
7 market
8 achieved

Grammar 1

Exercise 1
1 c 2 a 3 e 4 d 5 f 6 b

Exercise 2
1 b 2 c 3 b 4 c 5 a 6 c

Exercise 3
1 ✔
2 ✔
3 If you have financial problems, get some advice.
4 If I were you, I wouldn't buy that car.
5 If I could buy anything I wanted, I would buy a house in the country.
6 ✔
7 I can't afford to go to the cinema tonight unless Mum gives me some money.
8 Helen took her purse in case the bank was closed.
9 I'll buy it for you as long as you promise to use it.
10 ✔

Use of English: exam practice
1 UP
2 UNLESS
3 COME
4 BORROW
5 LITTLE / NO
6 IF
7 THAT
8 IN
9 TRY
10 WITHOUT
11 CASE
12 CLOSED

Reading: exam practice
1 C 2 A 3 D 4 E 5 B 6 A
7 E 8 B 9 D 10 C 11 A 12 E
13 B 14 D 15 C

Vocabulary

Exercise 1
1 borrow
2 lend
3 industry
4 economic
5 economical

Exercise 2
1 discount / credit card / bargains
2 currency / cheques
3 checkout / cashpoint
4 refund / receipt / change

Exercise 3
1 up
2 back
3 by
4 into
5 up
6 without

Use of English: exam practice
1 ADVERTISING / ADVERTISEMENTS
2 INCREASINGLY
3 CONSUMERS
4 LOYALTY
5 COMPETITION
6 SAVINGS
7 FASHIONABLE
8 STYLISH
9 INVESTMENT
10 FINANCIAL

Reading 2

Exercise 1

1 possess
2 see
3 hygiene
4 well-being
5 demands
6 influence

Exercise 2

1 agencies
2 consumers
3 regulations
4 ban
5 status
6 lifestyle

Grammar 2

Exercise 1

1 few
2 some
3 little
4 much
5 a
6 many

Exercise 2

1 I feel that I am lucky because I have a few friends who would lend me money if I needed it.
2 There is not much furniture in my room because I can't afford to buy things I like.
3 I went shopping this morning and bought a new pair of trousers / some new trousers.
4 You need to buy a piece of wood / some wood to fix that table.
5 ✔
6 I wonder if you could give me some advice about what MP3 player to buy?

Use of English: exam practice

Exercise 1

1 A 2 B 3 B 4 D 5 B 6 A
7 D 8 C 9 D 10 D 11 A 12 B

Exercise 2

1 ARE ONLY A FEW
2 HAS BEEN WORKING SINCE
3 SUCCEED IN PERSUADING
4 IF WE DON'T
5 I BORROW SOME MONEY FROM
6 AS LONG AS
7 COME UP WITH
8 HAVEN'T GOT A LOT

Listening: exam practice

1 A 2 B 3 C 4 A 5 C

Unit 5
Leisure

Reading 1

Exercise 1

1 e 2 h 3 a 4 g 5 b 6 d
7 f 8 c

Exercise 2

1 spent
2 nagging
3 missed
4 keeps
5 exasperating

Grammar 1

Exercise 1

1 ought
2 may
3 could
4 couldn't
5 have to
6 ought to

Exercise 2

1 AD 2 O 3 P 4 C 5 A 6 A

Exercise 3

1 had to
2 can't
3 should have
4 mustn't
5 don't have to
6 should

Use of English: exam practice

1 DIDN'T / DID NOT HAVE TO
2 SAID (THAT) WE COULD HAVE
3 CANNOT / CAN'T GET INTO / IN
4 WILL HAVE TO BE
5 CANNOT / CAN'T SPEAK
6 DON'T / DO NOT HAVE TO INVITE
7 TO BE ABLE TO
8 SHOULD HAVE TOLD

Reading: exam practice

1 C 2 H 3 A 4 F 5 B 6 D 7 E

Vocabulary

Exercise 1

1 spectator
2 cast
3 host
4 lifeguard
5 crowd
6 audience

Exercise 2

1 caught on
2 come round
3 flick through
4 take up
5 take to
6 get away

Exercise 3

1 activity
2 amusing
3 appreciation
4 Attendance
5 enjoyable
6 entrance
7 entertainment
8 excitement

Exercise 4
1 to get
2 in persuading
3 to organise
4 to meet
5 playing
6 to wear
7 go

Reading 2

Exercise 1
1 obstacles
2 twist
3 reasonable
4 notion
5 cable
6 current

Grammar 2

Exercise 1
1 most
2 than
3 biggest
4 worse
5 good
6 dramatically

Exercise 2
1 most expensive
2 better
3 least
4 longer, more interesting
5 more / less difficult
6 funniest

Exercise 3
1 Have you seen
2 Were you
3 did Sam do / has Sam done
4 decorated
5 didn't you call
6 is Sean going to invite

Exercise 4
1 most
2 that
3 Have
4 than
5 much
6 than
7 steep
8 as
9 most
10 Most
11 do you
12 you

Use of English: exam practice

Exercise 1
1 D 2 D 3 D 4 B 5 A 6 C
7 B 8 C 9 D 10 A 11 B 12 C

Exercise 2
1 OVER / ACROSS / AROUND / ROUND
2 THAN
3 THE
4 OF
5 ARE
6 BY
7 BE
8 LOOK
9 OTHER
10 LIKE
11 OF
12 FOR

Listening: exam practice
1 C 2 A 3 B 4 A 5 B

Unit 6
Nature

Reading 1

Exercise 1
1 bank
2 trickle
3 developing
4 conservation
5 population
6 processes
7 extinct
8 litter

Exercise 2
1 d 2 c 3 a 4 b

Exercise 3
1 Leaking
2 dam
3 Pollution
4 drought
5 protesting
6 Evaporation

Grammar 1

Exercise 1
1 Almost all the birds on the island have been killed by the cold weather.
2 People are being encouraged not to drop litter.
3 The government has been prevented from building a new reservoir by the local people.
4 Some dramatic news about the environment was announced yesterday.

Exercise 2
1 The problem of noise pollution is being studied by government scientists at the moment.
2 People need to be educated about the benefits of recycling.
3 A lot of water can be saved by turning the tap off when you are brushing your teeth.
4 A demonstration was held outside parliament yesterday to protest about air pollution.
5 A documentary on endangered species will be shown / is being shown on TV at eight o'clock tonight.
6 It has been announced that a new kind of environmentally friendly petrol will be produced / is being produced next year.

Exercise 3
1 have
2 are
3 being
4 be
5 been
6 was

Exercise 4
1 has been achieved
2 to be done / to do
3 have managed
4 have been threatened / were threatened
5 been saved
6 remains
7 has been made / is being made
8 have been solved

Reading: exam practice

1 A 2 C 3 D 4 D 5 C
6 A 7 B 8 A

Vocabulary

Exercise 1

1 out
2 off
3 down
4 out
5 away

Exercise 2

1 to
2 of
3 on, for
4 of
5 of / about

Exercise 3

1 system
2 species
3 effect
4 warming
5 reserve
6 fuels

Exercise 4

1 urban
2 smog
3 bring out
4 running out of
5 poisonous
6 Industrial

Use of English: exam practice

1 C 2 A 3 B 4 D 5 B 6 A
7 D 8 B 9 A 10 B 11 B 12 C

Reading 2

Exercise 1

1 b 2 c 3 a 4 c

Exercise 2

1 nomadic
2 tends
3 select
4 sole
5 critical
6 forage
7 infertile
8 intriguing

Grammar 2

Exercise 1

1 ✔
2 I wanted to write about zebras for the school project but my teacher wouldn't let me do it.
3 ✔
4 This factory stopped operating years ago because it was causing too much pollution.
5 It is important to turn off the tap when you are brushing your teeth because it wastes water.
6 It is my ambition to become a vet.
7 I would rather go to a natural history museum than a zoo.
8 You had better hurry up or we'll miss the bus to the waterfalls.
9 ✔
10 I prefer living in the country rather than in the city.

Exercise 2

(Suggested answers: Ensure that all students' answers contain the correct infinitive/*-ing* form)

1 ...to care about their environment.
2 ...destroying the Earth.
3 ...study geography than biology.
4 ...drop their litter in the street.
5 ...pay for damage they do to the environment.
6 ...pick wild flowers.
7 ...to learn about the dangers facing the environment.
8 ...by joining ecological organisations.

Use of English: exam practice

Exercise 1

1 SO
2 TO
3 HAVE
4 RATHER
5 THE
6 THEIR
7 MUCH
8 FROM
9 BE
10 IN
11 HAD
12 UP

Exercise 2

1 IS RUNNING OUT OF
2 HAD BETTER READ
3 AREN'T PEOPLE BEING INFORMED
4 SUCCEED IN CONVINCING
5 WAS FOUNDED
6 DEPEND ON US FOR
7 HAS BEEN ACCUSED OF BREAKING
8 TAKE CARE OF

Listening: exam practice

1 (local) councils / councils all over the country
2 factories
3 fossil fuels
4 nature reserves
5 within ten years

Revision 1

Reading: exam practice

1 F	2 C	3 D	4 B	5 C	6 E
7 B	8 D	9 F	10 A	11 E	12 B
13 C	14 D	15 D			

Use of English: exam practice

Exercise 1

1 D	2 B	3 D	4 C	5 C	6 A
7 C	8 B	9 D	10 B	11 B	12 C

Exercise 2

1 AROUND / OVER
2 OF
3 TO
4 AT
5 HAVE
6 EXAMPLE / INSTANCE
7 OUT
8 IN
9 AS
10 THAN
11 ORDER
12 TO / FOR

Exercise 3

1 TIRESOME
2 BEHAVIOUR
3 UNKIND
4 GUIDELINES
5 IMPROVEMENTS
6 RELATIONSHIPS
7 CREATIVE
8 ISOLATION
9 FREEDOM
10 HONESTY

Exercise 4

1 SUCH AN EXPENSIVE
2 TO AVOID USING
3 SUCCEED IN CONVINCING
4 WAS NOT / WASN'T ABLE TO GET
5 DID NOT / DIDN'T HAVE TO BRING
6 WERE YOU, I WOULD
7 WORK OUT HOW TO SOLVE
8 HAS BEEN TEACHING HERE FOR

Listening: exam practice

1 A 2 B 3 C 4 A 5 B

Unit 7
Sport

Reading 1

Exercise 1

1 stamina
2 balance
3 teamwork
4 agility
5 Freestyle
6 stunt

Exercise 2

1 taken off
2 skydiving
3 recreational
4 devoted
5 events
6 versions

Grammar 1

Exercise 1

1 feel
2 be
3 have been
4 have been
5 have been
6 like

Exercise 2

1 ought to bring / ought to be bringing
2 could be playing
3 should have remembered
4 could have gone
5 must have been
6 might have been delayed

Exercise 3

Students should have ticked sentences 1, 3 and 6

Use of English: exam practice

1 MUST HAVE BEEN
2 CAN'T / CANNOT HAVE SIGNED
3 MIGHT HAVE FORGOTTEN
4 COULD NOT HAVE BEEN
5 MAY BE RUNNING
6 MIGHT / MAY / COULD HAVE COME LAST
7 MUST BE GETTING
8 CAN'T / CANNOT MISS

Reading: exam practice

1 G 2 D 3 A 4 E 5 H 6 B 7 F

Vocabulary

Exercise 1

1 team
2 opponents
3 favourites
4 coaches
5 referee

Exercise 2

1 catch up
2 taking on
3 joined in
4 drop out
5 give up
6 put off

Exercise 3

1 loss
2 performance
3 injury
4 competitive
5 strength
6 preparation

Exercise 4

1 to go
2 to do
3 gone
4 play
5 went
6 is going / is going to go
7 play
8 to do

Reading 2

Exercise 1

1 b 2 d 3 e 4 a 5 c

Use of English: exam practice

1 C 2 B 3 D 4 C 5 D 6 A
7 B 8 C 9 B 10 A 11 C 12 D

Grammar 2

Exercise 1

1 at
2 on
3 in
4 in
5 at
6 on
7 in
8 at
9 on
10 at
11 in
12 in / at
13 on
14 in
15 at
16 in

Exercise 2

1 what time the game starts
2 how much the tickets are
3 where seat 43Z is
4 how I can meet the team afterwards
5 tell me if my friend Barry has arrived yet

Use of English: exam practice

Exercise 1

1 COMPETITION
2 PARTICIPANTS
3 PERFORMANCE
4 DECISION
5 PRECISION
6 TIMING
7 ACCURACY
8 PHOTOGRAPHY
9 FORTUNATELY
10 CERTAINTY

Exercise 2

1 MIND TELLING ME WHO IS
2 YOU THINK YOU COULD / WOULD / CAN
3 WONDER IF YOU COULD/CAN TELL
4 THEY ARRIVED AT
5 PREVENTED FROM PLAYING
6 STANDS FOR (THE)
7 ARE ALLOWED TO TAKE PART
8 A / ONE WEEK'S TIME

Listening: exam practice

1 C 2 F 3 A 4 B 5 D

Unit 8
Communication

Reading 1

Exercise 1

1 g 2 h 3 e 4 f 5 c 6 d
7 b 8 a

Exercise 2

1 deadlines
2 explosives
3 shoot
4 likeable
5 contribute
6 script

Grammar 1

Exercise 1

1 He said (that) he was tired of watching television.
2 She said (that) she was trying to listen to the news.
3 They said (that) they had sent a text message to Rachel.
4 She said (that) I had used up all the credit on her mobile.
5 She said (that) she had been trying to phone him for hours.
6 He said (that) he had been surfing the net the previous morning / the morning before.

Exercise 2

1 there
2 that day, the next day / the following day / the day after
3 the day before / the previous day
4 her, the following month / the next month / the month after
5 his, him
6 theirs

Exercise 3

1 Paul told me last week (that) he would be going on holiday the next day.
2 Last Saturday, Marsha said (that) she had had to work all day the day before.
3 David told Matt last month (that) he hoped / was hoping to visit him the following week.
4 On Sunday afternoon, Debbie said (that) she had been studying all morning.
5 When I saw Tina last week, she said (that) she was leaving for London that evening.
6 John told me yesterday (that) you were ill.

Use of English: exam practice

1 WAS NOT SURE HE WOULD
2 HAD NOT BEEN ABLE TO
3 SAID THAT THERE HAD BEEN
4 YEARS BEFORE HE HAD BEEN
5 I KNEW WHO HAD WRITTEN
6 FREE AT THAT MOMENT
7 WOULD CONTACT ME THE FOLLOWING
8 I HAD TO

Reading: exam practice

1 A/D 2 A/D 3 B 4 C 5 A 6 B 7 B
8 C 9 C 10 A 11 B 12 C 13 D
14 A/D 15 A/D

Vocabulary

Exercise 1
1 d 2 c 3 c

Exercise 2
1 turn
2 turn
3 hang
4 took
5 bring
6 putting

Exercise 3
About a year ago, I decided it was time to get a new television. My old one (which was almost an antique) had got damaged when we moved house and I could only get two or three channels clearly. But where was I going to get a new one? I got a bus into town and went straight to the electrical shop. When I got there, however, I got a shock. There were so many to choose from that I got lost inside the shop and I didn't know which one to get. They had got much more complicated over the years. They had also got bigger, which left me with another problem – how on earth was I going to get it home?

Use of English: exam practice

1 D 2 A 3 B 4 C 5 D 6 A
7 B 8 C 9 A 10 B 11 B 12 A

Reading 2

Exercise 1
1 emails
2 proportion
3 pioneer
4 merge
5 deleted
6 exceed
7 slump
8 instant

Exercise 2
1 video conferencing
2 subscribers
3 social networking sites
4 outmoded
5 phased out
6 unbeatable offers
7 appropriate

Grammar 2

Exercise 1
1 b 2 c 3 d 4 a

Exercise 2
1 He claimed to be / that he was an expert on computers but he nearly destroyed mine.
2 Despite the cost, I really want to get a laptop.
3 ✔
4 The thief denied stealing / having stolen my mobile.
5 ✔
6 They told me that the computer would cost a fortune to fix.
7 ✔
8 We agreed to pay half each for the phone bill.

Exercise 3
1 agree / refuse
2 suggest / deny
3 ask / tell
4 claim

Use of English: exam practice

Exercise 1
1 QUALIFICATIONS
2 COMMUNICATION
3 IMAGINATION
4 BELIEVABLE
5 CLOSELY
6 ENTHUSIASTIC
7 DISCUSSION
8 ARGUMENT
9 CONVERSATION
10 OBSERVATIONS

Exercise 2
1 SPITE OF THE FACT THAT
2 REFUSED TO SEND
3 SUGGESTED (MY) GIVING / (THAT) I (SHOULD) GIVE
4 OF (MY) NOT MAKING
5 SHE CLAIMED TO BE
6 TO DENY STEALING / HAVING STOLEN / THAT YOU STOLE
7 TOLD / ORDERED / COMMANDED HIM TO
8 EVEN THOUGH I HAVE TO

Listening: exam practice

1 C 2 B 3 C 4 A 5 C

Unit 9
Work

Reading 1

Exercise 1
1 g 2 d 3 b 4 a 5 e 6 f 7 c

Exercise 2
1 earned
2 position
3 errands
4 like-minded
5 straightforward
6 hire
7 income
8 franchise

Grammar 1

Exercise 1
Students should have ticked sentences 1, 4 and 5

Exercise 2
1 b 2 c 3 b 4 a 5 b 6 c

Exercise 3
1 e 2 c 3 b 4 f 5 a 6 d

Exercise 4
1 Jean and Toby, who are colleagues of mine, are coming to dinner tonight.
2 That office, which is Mr Phillipson's, is the biggest in the building.
3 Dave wasn't offered the job, which is a shame.
4 My new assistant, whose name is Gareth, seems very efficient.
5 The old factory, where Bob used to work, is for sale.
6 Tracy, who Elaine told me is leaving the company, didn't come to work today.

Reading: exam practice

1 D 2 F 3 A 4 H 5 C 6 B 7 E

Vocabulary

Exercise 1
1 g 2 i 3 a 4 l 5 f 6 k
7 e 8 j 9 b 10 h 11 d 12 c

Exercise 2
1 put in
2 fill in
3 took on
4 take over
5 takes up

Exercise 3
1 applicant
2 assistant
3 managing
4 training
5 supervisor
6 employees
7 worker

Exercise 4
1 made / had
2 doing
3 had
4 doing
5 making / taking
6 made
7 make
8 take / have
9 take

Reading 2

Exercise 1
1 c 2 e 3 f 4 a 5 d 6 b

Exercise 2
1 B 2 C 3 A 4 D 5 C 6 D
7 C 8 B 9 D 10 A 11 C 12 D

Grammar 2

Exercise 1
1 lifted
2 massaged
3 cut /done
4 dyed
5 done
6 made up

Exercise 2
1 eyes checked
2 dresses / shirts made
3 films developed
4 hair cut
5 dresses / shirts cleaned
6 car checked / cleaned / repaired

Exercise 3
1 We had / got a cherry tree removed from our garden (by Mr Fergus the farmer).
2 They had / got their garden wall rebuilt by three stone workers.
3 Mark and Julie had / got their wedding pictures taken by a professional photographer.
4 I had / got my subscription to *Nirvana* magazine renewed last week.
5 Having a Rolls-Royce repaired is very expensive.
6 My sister had / got her camera stolen yesterday.

Exercise 4
1 have / get her portrait painted
2 having / getting my hair dyed
3 had / got the TV repaired
4 is having / getting / is going to have / get her braces removed
5 (has) got / had her hours reduced
6 have / get that hat designed

Use of English: exam practice

Exercise 1
1 FOR
2 WHICH
3 MADE
4 FOR
5 MADE
6 IN
7 WHO
8 HAD
9 HOW
10 TAKE / ACCEPT
11 BY / ON
12 ON

Exercise 2
1 DO YOUR BEST
2 IS THE MAN WHOSE SISTER
3 TAKES UP TOO MUCH
4 GOT / WAS GIVEN THE SACK
5 HAVE THAT TOOTH TAKEN OUT
6 IS TAKING OVER
7 TAKE PART IN
8 THERE A LOT OF APPLICANTS

Listening: exam practice

1 university
2 characters
3 rejection letters / rejections
4 (lots of) determination
5 competition (for unpublished writers)

Unit 10
Health

Reading 1

Exercise 1
1 emergencies, panic, agony, hysterical
2 clutching, inadequate, hesitate, assessment
3 ran out, unconscious, bleeding, cope with
4 goes beyond, cuts and bruises, suppress, broken bones

Exercise 2
1 d 2 c 3 e 4 a 5 b

Grammar 1

Exercise 1
1 I didn't know about the restaurant. / I ordered a take-away.
2 You are wrong. / He isn't answering the phone.
3 You didn't tell me. / I didn't come.
4 Damian did something. / We are here now.

Exercise 2

1 d 2 a 3 f 4 b 5 e 6 c

Exercise 3
1 Had
2 have
3 had
4 been
5 If
6 would
7 Were
8 be
9 If
10 getting

Use of English: exam practice

1 FOR MY DOCTOR, I WOULD
2 HAD NOT / HADN'T KNOWN FIRST AID
3 NOT HAVE BEEN ILL IF
4 HAD I REALISED IT WAS
5 YOU TO SPEAK TO HIM
6 I WOULD BE ABLE
7 MIGHT NOT HAVE BEEN / GOT
8 WOULD NOT / WOULDN'T HAVE HAD

Reading: exam practice

1 D 2 B 3 B 4 C 5 A 6 C
7 B 8 D

Vocabulary

Exercise 1
1 to / round
2 up
3 down
4 out
5 out
6 over

Exercise 2
1 passed out, came to / round
2 broke out
3 come down with, cheer up
4 get over

Exercise 3
1 clinic
2 infection
3 check-up
4 tablets
5 germs

Exercise 4
1 Almost any doctor you see will advise you to give up smoking.
2 It's not like me to be ill – I'm usually so healthy.
3 It's not worth taking vitamins; just eat healthy food.
4 ✔
5 If you carry on working so hard, you're bound to get ill.
6 You cannot force children to eat vegetables.
7 ✔
8 My grandmother says there's no point (in) going to the doctor's.

Reading 2

Exercise 1
1 d 2 b 3 d 4 a

Exercise 2
1 demanding, commitment
2 scheme, designed
3 aspects, fascinating
4 Treating, care

Use of English: exam practice

1 VARIETY
2 TREATMENT
3 INJECTIONS
4 UNINVOLVED
5 RECOVERY
6 SURGEON
7 RESPONSIBILITY
8 OPERATION
9 SATISFACTION
10 ACTIVITIES

Grammar 2

Exercise 1

1 Could you make an appointment for me to see the doctor on Tuesday?
2 Why don't you lend him your book on health foods?
3 The doctor wrote me a prescription.
4 They told me that I might have to have a small operation.
5 I cancelled my meeting with Helen in order to go to the clinic.
6 You should eat healthily so as to avoid future problems.

Exercise 2

1 She showed the test results to me. / She showed me the test results.
2 In order to join the gym, you have to have this form signed by a doctor.
3 They gave the young mother an information sheet on childhood illnesses.
4 ✔
5 Show me exactly where you feel the pain.
6 I gave up junk food so as to / in order to try to lose some weight.

Use of English: exam practice

Exercise 1

1 GRANTED
2 NOT
3 ON
4 LIKE
5 BECOME/FALL
6 FEEL
7 US / YOU / ONE
8 GIVING
9 TO
10 IT
11 DOING
12 OF

Exercise 2

1 D 2 C 3 A 4 B 5 A 6 C
7 D 8 B 9 B 10 A 11 C 12 C

Listening: exam practice

1 B 2 A 3 C 4 A 5 C

Unit 11
Learning

Reading 1

Exercise 1

1 extracurricular
2 scholarship
3 break
4 report
5 playground
6 undergraduate

Exercise 2

1 e 2 d 3 c 4 a 5 f 6 b

Exercise 3

1 bright
2 recollections
3 debate
4 blossom
5 aid
6 traumatic

Grammar 1

Exercise 1

1 studied
2 were
3 didn't
4 passed
5 didn't / wouldn't show off

Exercise 2

1 had
2 wouldn't
3 could
4 hadn't failed
5 didn't

Use of English: exam practice

1 ONLY I DIDN'T HAVE
2 WOULD RATHER YOU DIDN'T
3 IF SHE GOT
4 (THAT) I LIVED CLOSER TO
5 ONLY I'D / I HAD BOUGHT
6 WISH YOU PAID / WOULD PAY MORE
7 (HIGH /ABOUT) TIME (THAT) YOU STARTED
8 IF MY DREAM CAME

Reading: exam practice

1 A 2 C 3 D 4 B 5 A 6 C
7 C 8 D

Vocabulary

Exercise 1

1 instructor
2 tutors
3 professors
4 teacher
5 apprentice
6 coach
7 trainee

Exercise 2

1 degree
2 skill
3 licence
4 certificate
5 exam result

Use of English: exam practice

1 C 2 D 3 A 4 B 5 B 6 D
7 A 8 C 9 B 10 D 11 B 12 C

Reading 2

Exercise 1

1 minute
2 fulfilled
3 armed
4 traumatised
5 highlights
6 satisfaction

Exercise 2

1 e 2 b 3 f 4 d 5 a 6 c

Grammar 2

Exercise 1

1 who were
2 who are
3 who are
4 which are

Exercise 2

1 Having studied
2 doing
3 Having tried
4 opening
5 Having paid
6 Having realised / Realising
7 Having completed

Exercise 3

1 coming
2 Hearing
3 sitting
4 being
5 Having

Use of English: exam practice

Exercise 1

1 BEEN
2 THAT
3 DO
4 THAN
5 HAVE
6 HAS
7 OF
8 TO
9 IN
10 WITH
11 WHICH
12 MORE

Exercise 2

1 ACADEMICS
2 EDUCATION
3 DECISION
4 ABILITIES
5 KNOWLEDGE
6 REFLECTION
7 PRACTICAL
8 INSTRUCTION
9 QUALIFICATION
10 SUCCESSFUL

Listening: exam practice

1 E 2 F 3 A 4 C 5 B

Unit 12
The Law

Reading 1

Exercise 1

1 on
2 between
3 in
4 for
5 on
6 to
7 from
8 on
9 on
10 to

Exercise 2

1 a rise in
2 lead to
3 was taken to court
4 stop him from doing
5 a cause for concern
6 has a negative impact on

Exercise 3

1 guilt
2 re-enacted
3 repercussions
4 reported
5 robbed

Grammar 1

Exercise 1

1 c 2 e 3 f 4 a 5 b 6 d

Exercise 2

1 do
2 had
3 do
4 did
5 are
6 have
7 are
8 have

Exercise 3

1 sooner had
2 did I realise
3 have I ever
4 Hardly
5 when
6 nor
7 Not
8 did
9 Only
10 was

Use of English: exam practice

1 HAD I GOT HOME WHEN
2 HAS THERE BEEN A BETTER
3 NO CIRCUMSTANCES WOULD I
4 DO YOU REALISE
5 HAD THE NEWS FINISHED THAN
6 NO TIME HAVE I
7 IS IT NECESSARY
8 WILL YOU BE ALLOWED TO

Reading: exam practice

1 B 2 C 3 E 4 D 5 B 6 E
7 A 8 D 9 C 10 B 11 A 12 E
13 D 14 A 15 C

Vocabulary

Exercise 1

1 e 2 a 3 c 4 b 5 g 6 d 7 f

Exercise 2

1 offenders
2 judge, jury
3 solicitor
4 witness
5 accused

Exercise 3

1 let off
2 went off
3 break in
4 made off
5 get away with
6 beaten up

Exercise 4

1 When the young girl was accused of stealing, she started to cry.
2 When they had collected enough evidence, the police finally charged the man with fraud.
3 Tim refused to help Stacey steal the sweets and ran home to tell his parents what she was planning to do.
4 Alan Halliwell, 27, was convicted of blackmail today at Manchester Crown Court.
5 ✔
6 Ray blamed his younger brother for breaking the window, but it wasn't really his fault.

Reading 2

Exercise 1

1 slogans
2 goods
3 theft
4 sentenced
5 majority
6 fraction

Exercise 2

1 B 2 C 3 A 4 D 5 B 6 C 7 B
8 D 9 A 10 C 11 C 12 B

Grammar 2

Exercise 1

1 b 2 d 3 g 4 a 5 e 6 h
7 f 8 c

Exercise 2

1 is known to be
2 is believed to be carrying
3 has been said that
4 is thought to be
5 not do it again, will
6 like the killer, do

Use of English: exam practice

Exercise 1

1 WHAT
2 OF
3 BEEN
4 TO
5 FOCUS / CONCENTRATE
6 ARE
7 SHOULD
8 OF
9 IN
10 IF
11 WILL
12 THE

Exercise 2

1 LAWYER
2 EVIDENCE
3 TRIALS
4 CRIMINALS
5 OFFENDER
6 THEFT
7 ROBBER
8 MURDERER
9 VIOLENCE
10 ACCUSED

Listening: exam practice

1 three-bedroom / 3-bedroom
2 six / 6 (o'clock)
3 a couple of / two / 2 months
4 (brand-new) (colour) TV
5 neighbours

Revision 2

Reading: exam practice

1 C 2 A 3 D 4 B 5 B 6 D
7 B 8 C

Use of English: exam practice

Exercise 1

1 D 2 B 3 B 4 A 5 C 6 B
7 C 8 D 9 A 10 B 11 C 12 D

Exercise 2

1 HAVE
2 WHO
3 THOSE
4 THEM
5 TO
6 WHERE
7 WERE
8 MADE
9 GOT
10 CLEANED / SWEPT
11 SPITE
12 DOES

Exercise 3

1 CRIMINAL
2 PUNISHMENT
3 OFFENCE
4 BENEFICIAL
5 COUNTLESS
6 HELPFUL
7 IMPROVEMENT
8 DECISION
9 DISCUSSION
10 EDUCATIONAL

Exercise 4

1 DENIED REPORTING ME
2 CIRCUMSTANCES SHOULD YOU GET
3 WOULD RATHER NOBODY TALKED
4 HAVE HIS TONSILS TAKEN OUT
5 WOULD YOU PASS ME THAT
6 (ME) WHETHER I WAS GOING
7 EVEN THOUGH
8 REFUSED TO COOPERATE

Listening: exam practice

1 B 2 C 3 B 4 A 5 B

Speaking Answer key

Unit 1

Exercise 1
1 Are you both still in full-time education?
2 What are your plans for the future?
3 What kind of things do you like doing in your spare time?
4 How long have you been living there?
5 What do you want to do when you leave school?
6 How long have you been studying English?

Exercise 2
1 Where
2 there
3 like
4 do
5 what
6 from
7 it
8 great
9 both
10 year
11 another
12 know
13 sure
14 decided
15 one
16 definitely

Unit 2

Exercise 1
1 need
2 away
3 bored
4 nerves
5 whereas
6 although

Exercise 2
1 first
2 other
3 Both
4 Another
5 difference
6 whereas
7 way
8 differ
9 On
10 on
11 far
12 away

Unit 3

Exercise 1
1 Would
2 fine
3 What
4 sure
5 like
6 point
7 about
8 agree
9 say
10 completely
11 sum

Exercise 2
1 b 2 d 3 a 4 e 5 c

Unit 4

Exercise 1
1 What kind of things do people buy on the internet? c
2 How do you feel about shopping in small shops? e
3 What are the advantages of shopping at large supermarkets? a
4 Have you ever bought anything at a street market? d
5 What are the disadvantages of shopping on the internet? b

Exercise 2
1 Both
2 In the first
3 The second
4 as
5 As for
6 On the one
7 On the other
8 Another point
9 while

Unit 5

Exercise 1
1 say
2 extremely
3 might
4 partly
5 What
6 certain
7 be
8 extent
9 suggest
10 should
11 Let's
12 without

Exercise 2
1 e 2 c 3 a 4 d 5 b

Unit 6

Exercise 1
1 me
2 I'm
3 opinion / view
4 ask
5 mind
6 view / opinion

Exercise 2
1 To
2 of
3 In
4 result
5 shows
6 say
7 similarity
8 If
9 concerned
10 my
11 It
12 no

Unit 7

Exercise 1

1 favourite
2 used
3 much
4 ambitions
5 enjoy

Exercise 2

1 c 2 d 3 a 4 e 5 b

Unit 8

Exercise 1

1 suggest
2 would
3 partly
4 about
5 afraid
6 say
7 be
8 sure
9 my
10 ask
11 example
12 true

Exercise 2

1 Do the media have a good influence on young people?
2 Do you try to keep up to date with the news?
3 Are too many violent images shown in the media?
4 What do you think is the best way to get the news?
5 Would you like to have a career in the media?
6 Do you think we should control what time certain programmes are shown?

Unit 9

Exercise 1

1 In
2 key
3 On
4 point
5 way
6 prefer

Exercise 2

1 with
2 of
3 like
4 shows
5 make
6 One
7 whereas
8 Another
9 similarity
10 both
11 Although
12 go
13 seems
14 definitely

Unit 10

Exercise 1

1 like
2 would
3 say
4 completely
5 What
6 certain
7 much
8 way
9 But
10 Lots
11 have
12 suggest
13 afraid
14 right

Exercise 2

1 e 2 c 3 a 4 b 5 d

Unit 11

Exercise 1

1 d 2 a 3 e 4 c 5 b

Exercise 2

1 tell
2 first
3 seem
4 other
5 worth
6 though
7 suppose
8 quite
9 hand
10 much
11 Personally
12 Sometimes
13 such
14 ask
15 have
16 although

Unit 12

Exercise 1

1 OK
2 mind
3 see
4 should
5 with
6 recommending
7 sure
8 Good
9 a
10 What
11 afraid
12 Another
13 Absolutely
14 should
15 go

Exercise 2

1 What are the main reasons people commit crimes?
2 What do you think it's like to be in prison?
3 Do you believe prison is the right punishment for most crimes?
4 Do you have a serious problem with crime in your area? / Do you have a problem with serious crime in your area?
5 Can you think of any other ways to prevent crime?

Audioscripts

Unit 1 Listening

1 Yeah, it was a real shame, because we used to be quite close. We don't really see each other these days. You know, I trusted him a lot, told him some things that I didn't tell most of my friends, and he let me down. It wasn't a huge amount, but he didn't stick to our agreement. In fact, he still hasn't paid me back completely. I've discussed it with other friends and they agree with me that it was unacceptable. He and I had a big argument about it, and that was that, really.

2 You don't really think about it when you're very young. Your twin is just there all the time. As you get older, though, you realise you're different from most people. I always had someone there who understood me and helped me. It could also be very funny, and people were often really embarrassed when they didn't know who was who. It wasn't always easy to get people to see me for who I was, rather than just one half of 'the Jones twins', but I wouldn't change it for the world, despite the difficulties.

3 Uh huh … yeah … well, things have been really busy at the office recently, and I haven't had time to go round and fix it. Maybe this weekend … uh huh … do you think so? Okay. I'll see what I can do, although I can't promise anything. Did you speak to Dad? What did he say? … Right. Well, Mum, you know, never even wanted it in the first place. I'll give you a call tomorrow and we'll arrange to go round, unless something comes up. All right, mate. Speak to you later.

4 He's fourteen now, and he's growing up so fast! It seems like only a few years since he was complaining about having to put his toys away. I always had to force him to do anything around the house! It was like one constant argument. He's completely different now. It's as if he's realised that I'm not just there to be his mum, and he understands that sometimes I've had a hard day at work. I see some other parents with their difficult teenagers who just give one-word answers to every question and I feel quite fortunate.

5 **Man:** So how are things going?
Woman: Oh, can't complain. I suppose. Everyone's fine. I've been working a lot, and my boss is making life difficult, but that's nothing new.
Man: Oh, mine can be like that. It's an old family business and they're very traditional. I keep making suggestions, but the brothers who run it never listen. You're at Walker's, aren't you?
Woman: That's right. In the accounts department. Nearly six years now. Oh, there's my bus. Nice to see you again. Say hello to your sister from me.
Man: I will.

Unit 2 Listening

Interviewer: I'm in the Australian city of Perth, and with me is Rita Wentworth, who works as a tour guide in and around the city. Now, Rita, first of all, could you tell us a little about the city?

Rita: Sure. Well, Perth has been here since it was started by Captain James Stirling, back in 1829. There were native Australians in the area before that, but that was when the British first arrived. And unlike other cities, such as Sydney, whose first residents were mostly prisoners from Britain, the people who first lived in Perth were free. They came to Australia from Britain to make a better life for themselves and their families.

Interviewer: What's Perth like today?

Rita: It's a very large city of over 1.5 million people, so there's lots to do and lots to see. It's on the coast, so of course lots of people go surfing in the area, but away from the beaches there are some very interesting parts of the city. Art lovers will be interested in the West Australian Art Gallery, which often has modern art exhibitions, and there's lots for music lovers too at the Perth Concert Hall. And Perth is famous for its sports.

Interviewer: Really?

Rita: Oh, yes. The local cricket team is very popular, and so is the Australian rules football team – you know, that's a game like rugby that we play in Australia. There's also a lot of support for the Perth Wildcats, the basketball team. And there are a lot of facilities for local people, and visitors, to play sports themselves.

Interviewer: Thanks, Rita. Now, I'm going to speak to some local people to find out what they think about living…

Unit 3 Listening

Speaker 1: I wanted a digital camera for Christmas because my friend was coming to stay with me and I wanted to take some photos. My husband said he would get me one, and he did. Well, I've never been really very good with modern technology, and I hadn't used one before. I took some photos during the Christmas holiday and let my husband put them on the computer. When we saw them, though, the quality wasn't very good. It was a bit disappointing, but it seems I had it on the wrong setting. I should have studied the book that came with it, but I don't have the patience for that kind of thing.

Speaker 2: I needed a new laptop, so I went along to my local shopping centre and had a look at what they had there. I found one I liked and asked a shop assistant to show it to me. It seemed okay, but he said that I would really need something faster and that had many more features. In the end, I spent more money and got one that is much more powerful than I really need. I wish I'd just got the one I liked.

Speaker 3: I had a problem with a dishwasher. After I got it, a friend told me that you have to clean the filter in the bottom and add special salt to it. I hadn't known that, but I thought it should be easy. You just take the filter out, clean it and put it back. Then there's a place to put the salt. I did it and left the filter to dry. When I came back later, it had gone. Couldn't see it anywhere. I've got no idea what happened, but now the dishwasher doesn't work properly.

Speaker 4: I've got a new mobile phone now, but it's the first new one I've had for about five years. My last one was quite old and didn't have all these complicated features that new ones do. People kept telling me to get a new one, but I never seemed to have enough money at the right time. To be honest, my friends started to make fun of it, so I stopped taking it out with me and left it at home – which is a bit of a waste of time with a mobile! I'm much happier with this one.

Speaker 5: My dad always says that the cheap one will cost you more money in the end, and I realise now that he's right. I got a microwave, and I tried to spend as little money as I could. When I got it home, I realised that there weren't any instructions and no guarantee. It stopped working after a week, and I had to take it back to the shop. They gave me another, and that developed a problem within a couple of months. Finally, I paid more for a better one.

Unit 4 Listening

Interviewer: Hello, and welcome to the *Money Show*. I'm joined today by Tessa Crowe, who is a financial expert, and we're talking about money problems. Tessa, tell us what kind of problems people come to you with.

Tessa: Well, it varies. My customers sometimes want advice about which bank account is best for them and sometimes they want to know about investing money. The biggest category is probably money owed on credit cards, though. Many people use them to buy things, and later they realise that after paying their household bills they don't have enough money left to pay back what they've borrowed. It's a problem that seems to be increasing.

Interviewer: And how does that happen?

Tessa: Credit cards work on a 'buy now, pay later' basis. So when people are thinking of buying something, let's say a new pair of shoes or the latest bit of modern technology, they are thinking about what they want, not what they can afford. When they look at the price tag, they think it's okay to go for the more expensive one because they don't have to pay for it immediately. Unfortunately, though, if they do that too often, they end up with a large monthly bill.

Interviewer: What's your advice?

Tessa: First of all, if you're concerned about your credit card bills, don't just sit there and worry and try to ignore them. One thing the credit card companies hate is not knowing what's happening. Before you get in touch with someone like me, call them and explain the situation. They may be able to help. If they're not very helpful, then it's time to speak to your bank manager, or maybe an adviser like me.

Interviewer: And what can you do for people?

Tessa: When I sit down with people, the first thing I do is explain that I can't wave a magic wand and make it all disappear. But I can at least stop it getting bigger. I tell them to stop using their cards immediately. Many people just put them away somewhere, perhaps in a locked drawer, but I prefer my customers to cut them up, so that there's no chance of them being used again. Then we work out how much they can afford to pay back.

Interviewer: What happens to people after they see you?

Tessa: Most of them manage to sort their problem out and eventually pay off the money they owe, and they might even start using a card sensibly again. Of course, there are a few who find themselves in the same situation a year or two later. It's very hard to know how to help those people. For some, credit cards are just too tempting and it's just too easy to spend a lot of money.

Interviewer: Tessa Crowe, thanks for coming to talk to us today.

Unit 5 Listening

1 That sounds great. We haven't done that for a long time. Do you remember what happened last time? Yeah, that was funny. Danny tried to kick it like a football and hurt himself. In the end, though, he was really good at knocking them down, wasn't he? It'll make a change from losing to him at pool every weekend, anyway. You contact everyone and see if they want to join us for coffee afterwards, at that place round the corner.

2 My husband got the tickets, and it had been ages since we went to the theatre, so I was really looking forward to it. I don't know if you've been to the Royal Theatre, but they've changed it recently. Do you remember? It used to be really cold and uncomfortable until they modernised it. We had seats near the front, so we could see everything. The performance looked great, and I loved the dresses the women were wearing. The only thing that spoiled it was that some of the people on stage … I just wasn't convinced by their performance, really. I thought they were quite bad and needed more training.

3 No … on the sixteenth … that's right, Mr Reeves, Gordon Reeves … and we're in seats 35F and 35G … have you found it? Right, well, the thing is that I've got my brother and his wife visiting then, and I realised that they don't have tickets, so I was wondering whether there are any left … oh … right … that's a shame. We'll have to go on the following Friday, then … yes, if you can change those, that's great ... and the seats are 35F and G. Right … thank you.

4 We saw it on DVD last night. What a load of rubbish! I just don't believe that a man like that would leave his job and go and live in the country. And then meet the girl of his dreams. I did think their relationship was handled quite well in the end, I suppose, but the plot was so simple and predictable that I started falling asleep. I prefer films that are more true to life, where people have understandable reasons for doing things. I wasn't impressed.

5 I don't play video games so often, but someone got me this one for my birthday, so I tried it out. It's great! The idea is that you're trying to rescue a princess, and you have to fight lots of monsters to get to her. It might look a bit old-fashioned, but I loved the bits where you have to fight. You have to be really quick on the controls, but when you do it right, it's awesome. The background music can get a bit annoying, but that's not a major problem. You should come round and play it some time.

Unit 6 Listening

Interviewer: Today on *Nature Watch*, we're talking about the local environment and what we can all do to help protect it. We'll be talking to local people to get their opinions, but first I'm talking to Robert Jackson. Robert, why don't you start by telling us what exactly you do.

Robert: Well, I'm a scientist and I travel all over the country and I speak to local councils to help them develop their environmental programmes. This means that I study the local needs and the local problems and try to come up with ideas that councils can use to deal with the problems.

Interviewer: And what problems have you been looking at in our area?

Robert: This area is quite interesting because there used to be a lot of factories in the past. These have mostly been replaced now by shopping centres or by housing for local people, but there are still some pollution problems left behind.

Interviewer: What kind of problems?

Robert: These places often burned a lot of fossil fuels, which of course adds to global warming, but there's not much we can do about that at a local level. However, many of them gave off chemicals that can still be found in the soil or even in some rivers. One of my jobs is to help the council find ways to get rid of those chemicals and help nature recover in those areas.

Interviewer: What kind of things do you suggest?

Robert: There are really two main stages. The first is to clean the soil and water using filters and special chemicals. Then we need to build nature reserves to protect the area and to allow nature to do the rest of the job. You know, nature is very good at recovering from this kind of thing, as long as we give it the chance to. With proper management, any areas affected by this kind of pollution should be back to normal within ten years. Part of my job is to follow that process and check that everything is going well.

Interviewer: Thanks, Robert, for telling us about what you do. Now let's listen to the opinions of a few local people.

Revision Unit 1 Listening

1 I realised I had some free time on my hands, and I wanted to do something useful for my local area, so I got involved in an environmental scheme. It's run by the local council. They come up with a plan for which areas need cleaning up, and we do it. It's very varied – last week it was a beach, this week it's a river. None of us get paid, it's purely voluntary, and it's not easy for everyone to spare the time, but we're all very proud of what we do. I wish I'd got involved years ago, because it's a great feeling to know that you're making a difference.

2 In the end I stopped going to German lessons, so I'll have to find something else to do with my weekend. I don't know. It was fun for a while, and I met some nice people. It just became harder to justify the expense when the course fees went up, and I knew there wasn't much chance of me going there on holiday. I was just learning for personal interest, and I think I got what I wanted. Now, for example, I could probably read a novel in German, as long as I had my dictionary with me. So I'm looking for something else, preferably something free. Any suggestions?

3 In my opinion, we are all too eager to accept modern technology and everything it brings. Companies bring out the latest thing and we all rush out and buy it, without really thinking about it. The main problem is that we start to believe that we can have everything without making an effort. We spend a relaxing evening online, and in order to communicate with people on the other side of the world, all we have to do is press a few buttons. We come to think that anything that isn't available to us instantly and easily is a waste of time, and I think that's the real problem.

4 Oh, it was so annoying! What happened was, I was going to stay over at Emma's place, and I told my mum we were going to revise for the exam, which was true. She rang Emma's mum to check that everything was all right and that I could go over, but it turned out that Emma was in trouble for not doing something, the washing up, I think. Anyway, that meant I couldn't go round. She's always doing things like that. It's so annoying!

5 I've always loved insects, ever since I was a little boy. There are so many different kinds that you could spend your whole life studying them and still only know a tiny amount. They manage to find a way to live almost anywhere on Earth, even in places where lots of other things can't, and that's what I find most impressive about them. Whether it's social species like ants, which work together to build a large colony, or solitary species who live on their own, you'll find an insect almost everywhere you look. Isn't that amazing?

Unit 7 Listening

Speaker 1: Well, we did rugby in the winter, football in the spring and cricket in the summer. And that was about it, really. Whatever the weather, that's what we played. I was quite good at cricket, actually. I was captain of the school team in my last year. I wish we'd done the kind of things my kids do today. You know, canoeing, karate, aerobics, cycling, that kind of thing, but it was only a small school, and they just didn't have the facilities, more's the pity.

Speaker 2: I went to rather an unusual school where we were encouraged not to see sport in terms of winning or losing. I think the head teacher didn't like the idea of competition. We did play hockey and tennis, but only for fun, really, and I remember being really jealous of children at other schools who, if they were good enough, had the chance to play in the school team. We didn't have any, you see. As far as I remember, we didn't even have a school sports day. Though I do remember going on cross-country runs when it was too wet to play hockey. We'd all run in a group – no winners again, you see! – and we'd all come back soaked. I think we all quite enjoyed that, really.

Speaker 3: It's only in the last five years or so that I've discovered the pleasures of doing sport. I hated it at school. I think it's because we were forced to do it. I'm the kind of person who enjoys things they choose to do, but resents being made to do something. Especially playing football in the rain. Anyway, I know most of the kids used to really look forward to two hours of games every afternoon, but I used to dread it. At least I never ended up in a school team. That would have been awful!

Speaker 4: Do you know what really put me off sport at school? It was the fact that such a great emphasis was placed on being good. Do you know what I mean? I think these days, it's all about taking part and having fun, and who cares how many goals you score? At my school it wasn't like that at all. The kids who made it into the school teams were worshipped by the other kids – and by the teachers, to tell you the truth – and the other kids, like me, who weren't particularly good, well, we were looked down on.

Speaker 5: I think I'd have enjoyed it all a lot more if it hadn't always been so cold and wet. I went to school in Tavistock in Devon, which is famous for its dreadful weather. It was either pouring with rain, or the ground was frozen hard. Horrible! I remember once, near the start of term, I was tackled in a game of rugby. I landed badly, and broke my arm. I couldn't do any sport for the rest of term, and I remember feeling so relieved that I wouldn't have to stand out there on the rugby pitch shivering for two hours like my friends!

Unit 8 Listening

Presenter: Susan Blake joins me now to talk about the newspaper *The Daily Post*, which was launched this week. Susan, we've seen four issues of *The Daily Post* now. Is it going to be a success, do you think?

Susan: Well, that's actually a very difficult question, and I think the only real answer is that time will tell. But, I do think they've got off to a good start, and I gather that the two million people who bought yesterday's copy tend to agree.

Presenter: So, what are they doing right, in your opinion?

Susan: Well, to start with, I think people like the fact that this is the size of a typical tabloid newspaper – it's not difficult to hold when you're standing on a train or bus, for example – but that there is actually quite a lot of news in it. You know, real news, not just stories about celebrities and soap stars. Secondly, a lot of newspapers only really appeal to people in their forties and fifties. You know, people with houses and families and quite good jobs. *The Daily Post* seems to be aimed at a younger audience too. I can imagine some teenagers reading it, and students, and people in their twenties and thirties. There's still plenty for people who are in their forties or older, of course, too.

Presenter: Now, many newspapers side with one political party against the other parties. Do you get the feeling *The Daily Post* does that too?

Susan: Well, they certainly claim that they're politically independent, and judging from the first four issues, I think that's probably true. They've attacked the government on some things, and supported them on others. We'll see if that changes over the next few months. I suspect it might.

Presenter: Right. Are there any things you don't like about the paper?

Susan: There are definitely some things they can improve. They've only got one page for the day's TV schedule, which isn't really enough. It would be a lot easier to read if it was spread over two pages. Also, they're going to be producing a free magazine every Tuesday called *The Tuesday Magazine*. We saw the first one yesterday, and that really was a bit poor. I know it's just an extra that you get with the paper, but it was so full of adverts, it was actually difficult to find any articles in it. They'll have to do better than that, I'd say.

Presenter: One final question. Do you think the other newspapers should be worried?

Susan: Yes, I do. They're definitely going to see their sales drop as people switch to *The Daily Post*. They're going to have to try hard to get them to come back, but I'm sure they will try. I imagine in a couple of months or so the other papers will drop their prices a little to encourage people to buy them again.

Unit 9 Listening

Presenter: Joining me in the studio today is the well-known author Craig Danton. Craig, welcome to the show. Thanks so much for coming in today.

Craig: You're very welcome!

Presenter: Craig, your latest novel, *The Forgotten Children*, has sold over a million copies and these days you're a highly respected writer. Was it easy to get your first novel published?

Craig: My first novel? To be honest, I didn't even try to get that published! I wrote it when I was a university student, and, once I'd finished it, put it away in a drawer and started on the next one.

Presenter: Really? Do you think you'll publish it at some time in the future?

Craig: No, no. It really wasn't very good at all. I don't think I developed the characters properly, and the plot was a bit weak, to tell you the truth. But the thing about being a writer is that the more you write, the better you get, so it wasn't a waste of time. Without it, I couldn't have written my second novel.

Presenter: And that was *Darkness at Midday*?

Craig: *Darkness at Midday*, that's right.

Presenter: And how easy was it to get that published?

Craig: Well, it took me about three years! When I finished it, I sent it off to a publisher in London. A few months later, they politely replied that it wasn't for them, so I sent it to another one. And the same thing happened again and again and again.

Presenter: How many rejection letters did you get in total?

Craig: Seventeen!

Presenter: There must have been times when you wanted to give up, when you thought, 'I'm never going to get this book published.'

Craig: There were definitely times when I thought that, but no, I never wanted to give up. There are so many stories of successful books being turned down initially, you just need lots of determination to keep going. If the book's good enough, you'll find a publisher in the end.

Presenter: Like you did.

Craig: Yes. Well actually, for that book, I entered it into a competition for unpublished writers and it won first place. From that moment on, publishers were queuing up to publish it!

Unit 10 Listening

1 I was about fifteen or sixteen, I suppose. It had never crossed my mind to become a nurse before then, even though my mum was one. I don't think I ever really knew what she did, to be honest, though I guess I'd watched hospital dramas on TV. Anyway, I had to go into hospital for an operation, and this nurse was just really kind and friendly and I thought: 'That's the kind of job that I'd like to have.' Mum gave up nursing a few years ago now, and I think she's rather pleased I've chosen the same job she had.

2 Certainly at the hospital where I work a lot has been spent on new equipment over the past few years, and in that respect I think we're one of the best hospitals in the whole region. Having said that, though, I can really only give a patient coming to see me about ten minutes for an initial consultation. Fifteen minutes maximum. So I think it often feels to the patient like it's all a bit rushed, which is a shame. We do have a lot of forms to fill in, of course, but that's just part of the job, really, and you have to find time for it somehow.

3 The thing is, Debbie, I know you really want to go on this diet, but you're actually not overweight at all and I don't really know anything about it. They're always warning people not to go on special diets without talking to a doctor first, so how about we make an appointment for you to see Dr Marshall? If he says it's okay, then we can talk about it further.

4 For about three days before I went, I was really scared. It's silly, isn't it, but I'd just got it into my head that it would be really painful and I'd have to sit in the chair for ages and it would just be a really unpleasant thing. Well, when I got there, he was so friendly and just put me at my ease, that I didn't even mind when he said I had to have three fillings. It was clear he knew what he was doing, and I was just happy to let him get on with his job.

5 **Vet:** So, what seems to be the problem with old Buggles, here?
Boy: Well, I'm not sure, but something's not quite right. Usually he spends several hours a day running round the living room, but he hasn't done that recently. If you look in his eyes, it's like he's a bit sad or something. Depressed. He just sits there.
Vet: I see. What about his eating habits? Have they changed at all?
Boy: Let me think. No, he's still eating the same amount each day. Yeah, that hasn't changed.

Unit 11 Listening

Speaker 1: I took my driving test about twenty years ago, and it really was the strangest experience ever. I was driving along, doing what I was told. You know, 'turn left at the end of the road, then take the next right.' That kind of thing. When all of a sudden the examiner shouted 'Stop!' I didn't know what I'd done wrong. A man ran up to the car, and said his wife was really ill and had to get to the hospital now. Well, we took them. I didn't actually know the way to the hospital, so all the way it was 'turn left at the end of the road'! I did drive faster than you do in the normal test, though. We got there okay and the examiner said it had been the most unusual test he'd ever been involved in. I passed!

Speaker 2: I'd just moved to Scotland, and really needed a car where I lived, so I decided to have lessons. They were fine, but when it came to the test, the person testing me had a really, really broad Scottish accent, and I just couldn't make out anything he said. Every time he gave me an instruction, I had to ask him to repeat it at least three times. He was very kind, though, and didn't penalise me for that, thank goodness.

Speaker 3: I was so nervous in my test and I made a really stupid mistake. We'd been driving around for about three minutes when the examiner said 'I'd like you to turn left at the T-junction up ahead.' Now, I know the difference between left and right, and I did hear him clearly say 'left', but for some reason which I'll never understand – I guess I just wasn't thinking clearly – I indicated to go right, and actually turned right at the T-junction. I failed that time, but passed the next time I took the test.

Speaker 4: I suppose it's what everyone dreads happening in their test – and it happened to me. We'd just started the test and I was changing gear – I think I was going from first to second gear – when the gear stick came right off in my hand. I couldn't believe it! It was totally broken. It wasn't my fault, of course, and the examiner was very good about it. We had to start the test again in a different car.

Speaker 5: I was in a panic when I took my test. The whole day had gone badly, and I nearly didn't make it to the test centre on time. Anyway, I definitely wasn't relaxed at all, and we were doing that bit where you have to reverse around a corner. So what did I do? I drove straight into a parked car. I didn't do a lot of damage – there was just a tiny bump really – but it was enough for me to fail the test, of course.

Unit 12 Listening

Woman: And in other news today, a bizarre burglary in Leeds has left police baffled. Joseph and Mary Carter woke up yesterday morning to find that all the doors and windows of their three-bedroom house in the Wakefield district of the city had been stolen. Toby Marsh tells us more.

Toby: Before Joseph and Mary Carter went to bed last night, they shut the windows and locked the front door as usual. But when they woke up this morning, they were gone.

Mary: I got up first, at about six o'clock, and I pulled back the curtains in the bedroom, and this cold blast of air hit me. The window had gone. I woke Joseph, and that's when we discovered what had happened.

Joseph: We couldn't believe it. We didn't hear a thing in the night. How on earth could someone take all the doors and windows of our house without us hearing a thing? It doesn't make sense. The worst thing is we only had them fitted a couple of months ago. They were brand new.

Toby: Police officers on the scene are baffled.

Police officer: It's one of the strangest crimes I've ever witnessed, and I've been on the force for over fifteen years. There are so many things about this we don't understand.

Why would someone take all the doors and windows? How did they do it so quietly? Why didn't they take anything else? The Carters had a brand-new colour TV in the living room. That's still there. It's quite peculiar.

Toby: Officers are currently interviewing neighbours in the hope that someone saw or heard something. Meanwhile, Joseph and Mary Carter are boarding up their windows and doors until they can be replaced.

Revision Unit 2 Listening

Presenter: In the news again this week is another story about language and genetics. Scientists are claiming they have more evidence for there being a 'language gene'. So, I'm glad to have Carol Dickinson, Professor of Linguistics at Charleston University in the studio with me to try to make sense of all this. Carol, thanks for coming in.

Carol: My pleasure.

Presenter: Carol, the idea that there's a specific gene in our bodies that gives us language strikes many of us as being a bit silly. Can it possibly be true?

Carol: Yes, it does seem silly, doesn't it? The problem is often with the way this is reported. Journalists take something a scientist has said, and report it as something entirely different. We both speak English. People in Japan speak Japanese. Now clearly it's nothing to do with genetics, with our DNA, that we speak English and they speak Japanese. Which language you speak is purely down to environmental factors.

Presenter: So, if it's nature versus nurture, it's nurture that determines what language we speak?

Carol: That's right, and that's just common sense. What scientists have been asking for a while now, though, is why do humans acquire language so easily, whereas other animals, apes for example, don't? And what the evidence suggests is that there is something in our DNA, in our genes, that gives us the ability to pick up language. And that's what some people call 'the language gene', although of course it may be more than one gene that helps it all happen.

Presenter: But, what you seem to be talking about – a language gene – if it's true, then it applies to all languages in the world, right?

Carol: That's right.

Presenter: But – and maybe I'm wrong here – languages are very, very different. How can there be something in all of us that can enable us to learn so many different languages? Do you see what I mean? Chinese has a totally different set of grammatical rules to English, doesn't it?

Carol: That's actually a really interesting, and important question. If you're right, if there are languages in the world that have absolutely nothing in common, then it's unlikely that there's a language gene in all of us. But what we've found is that in fact all the languages in the world do share a large number of characteristics.

Presenter: For example?

Carol: Well, for example, all human languages have nouns, verbs and adjectives. And all languages follow certain rules. If I say to you 'You are a radio presenter', in English we can make that a question by swapping round the subject and the verb: 'Are you a radio presenter?' Other languages do it differently, of course, but there isn't a single language in the world where they make a question by reversing the word order of the whole sentence: 'Presenter … radio … a … are … you?'. So all languages follow quite strict rules, which we sometimes call 'the universal grammar'. The differences are minor in comparison. It's been said, and I agree with this, that if a Martian came down to Earth, he'd think we all spoke the same language, with just a few minor regional differences.